UNBREAKABLE

Book One

WRONG PLACE, WRONG TIME...

A TRUE ACCOUNT OF A YOUNG INDIAN BOY LIVING IN AN ERA OF RACIAL HATRED

Jag Singh

www.jagsingh.uk

MINTER PUBLISHING LIMITED

Minter Publishing Limited (MPL)
Cheltenham UK

Copyright © Jag Singh 2020, 2025

Jag Singh has asserted his rights under the Copyright, Design, and Patents Act, 1988
to be the author of this work.

First edition published by Minter Publishing Limited in 2020

This revised edition was published by Minter Publishing Limited in 2025

Paperback ISBN: 978-1-910727-57-7

Cover Design by James Minter.

Printed and bound in Great Britain by Ingram Spark, Milton Keynes.

This book is sold subject to the condition that it shall not, by way of trade or otherwise, be lent, resold, hired out, or otherwise circulated in any form of binding or cover other than that in which it is published and without a similar condition, including this condition, being imposed on the subsequent purchaser.

The story is based on actual events. Names, characters, places, and incidents have been altered or renamed for legal purposes and are used fictitiously. Any resemblance to actual persons, living or dead, events, or locales is entirely coincidental.

What People are saying about
UNBREAKABLE

Powerful, authentic, and important. Great piece of work by the author at a time when we really need to understand the impact of racism and bullying in our culture. The best way for change is to understand the lived experiences of those who have suffered and it's about time a book like this was written. **A S Malhotra**

Inspiring, funny, sad and everything in between. This has to be made into a film! I didn't stop reading once I started. This has every emotion you can have in a lifetime! Great read!
Kelly Barnes

Amazing book! Jag has done an incredible job in making the reader truly understand what it must've been like in those harsh times. Would recommend this to everyone.
Mandeep Singh Diraag

Touching story, a must-read. Perfect for education on discrimination and racism. A great case study and very moving. Well written, an easy but emotional read. JAG Singh is inspiring, and I'm looking forward to more from him.
Sophie Outen

An insightful and at times, terrifying memoir about growing up as a minority in 1970s London. A true story of bravery and survival. I would and will be recommending this to everyone and can't wait for the next instalment.
Carol Hughes

DEDICATION

In loving memory of our Sweet 'Auntie Polly,' thank you so much for teaching us the True Power of Perseverance.

If it isn't written, it will ultimately be forgotten. People will never know that such events took place, even though the story was worth remembering... forever.

— JAG SINGH

CONTENTS

PREFACE I
INTRODUCTION 1
CHAPTER 1 THIS TOO SHALL PASS 9
CHAPTER 2 HARD GRAFT 20
CHAPTER 3 CANNING TOWN 35
CHAPTER 4 RULE, BRITANNIA! 40
CHAPTER 5 LITTLE INDIA: 1977 53
CHAPTER 6 FROM BAD TO WORSE 61
CHAPTER 7 INTIMIDATION 84
THE 'UNBREAKABLE' SAGA CONTINUES... 101
FOR PARENTS, TEACHERS, & GUARDIANS: 124
ABOUT THE 'UNBREAKABLE' TRILOGY 125
ABOUT THE AUTHOR 127
ACKNOWLEDGEMENTS 128
SUPPORT GROUPS 131
SOCIAL MEDIA 132

PREFACE

It wasn't easy for me to write these memoirs. It meant reliving those gruesome days of my childhood by picturing them again in my head. As I began to write, the nightmares and memories of the bullying and mental abuse suffered all those years ago came rushing back. Though troubled, I continued to write as I felt a real need to tell people my story, and to send out the empowering message that no matter what, we must all find ways to live together in peace and harmony on our beloved planet, our home, our Earth. I believe it's possible and can be done; it is up to us.

While writing these memoirs, I was constantly reminded of the horrific experiences I'd encountered during the nineteen seventies, yet I felt a profound relief that they were over. The hate crimes, the bullying, and the brutal racism that my family and I witnessed are now part of history. The storm had passed; although it left many mental scars, it has finally ended. As a family, we struggled through those ghastly years in East London and somehow survived.

As a young man, I spent many years trying to ignore the negative experiences of my childhood, as many people do, but it proved ineffective. When I reached adulthood, I realised I had to take positive action to prevent younger generations from being treated in the same way. Having been bullied for most of my school life, I had first-hand experience of the gruelling effects this behaviour has on a child, both mentally and physically. Ultimately, I resolved to use my negative past as motivation; I became determined and empowered to raise awareness and help stop the vicious cycle from continuing.

Initially, I stood before hundreds of children at various school assemblies and spoke about child protection and anti-bullying. Knowing I was helping children avoid unhappiness, stay safe, enjoy school, and learn to be respectful brought me immense satisfaction and fulfilment. I felt I was making a difference, thereby healing myself in the process.

Visiting the schools was just the beginning; I have since conducted motivational interviews on television and radio, hosting my own inspirational shows to encourage and empower audiences to lead fulfilling lives. I have derived a great deal of pleasure and satisfaction from these appearances and will endeavour to continue this journey for as long as possible.

INTRODUCTION

THE 14TH DECEMBER, 1980, IS ETCHED into my mind and will be forever. There I was, a mere ten-year-old boy, totally astounded by what I saw in front of me with my very own eyes. Standing barefoot on the pavement, with my head tilted back and mouth gaping, I watched as the violent rages of fire consumed the very essence of my home without mercy or hesitance. Engulfed in flames and with thick black acrid smoke roaring through the chimney toward the dark red midnight sky, my home soon disappeared to become a burnt-out shell, a pile of rubble, a heap of smouldering detritus. It was at this point that I made myself a promise that I would go on to complete at a later age. In essence, it was to do whatever I could to prevent 'hate-crime', to support 'anti-bullying', raise 'mental health' awareness and strive to make the world a better place. Nobody's house should be decimated by fire because of their skin colour, religious beliefs, or cultural background. And certainly, neither child nor adult should have to witness their home being destroyed as I did on that frightful night.

As the surrounding bystanders mumbled

away, some noticed that I was only wearing my pyjamas on this freezing, wintry night. A tall, middle-aged woman came running up and wrapped me from behind with her long, fluffy seventies-fashioned green Maxi coat. At first, I didn't even realise what she was doing, I was too busy thinking: *how the hell was I still alive?*

I'll never forget what this caring white English woman said to me, "Oh come 'ere me lovely... You poor little boy."

It just wasn't normal to find a family standing outside their house watching it burn away. I found it so hard to believe that this unknown white stranger had so much loving concern for me. I wasn't used to such behaviour from the White-British individuals, rather the total opposite.

Dumbfounded by what was happening to our house, I don't even remember feeling the coldness of the night. In fact, I couldn't feel anything. My thoughts and focus were on our house as the uncontrollable fire raged through room after room.

At that time, I wasn't sure how I was going to live up to the promise I had just made to myself, but that didn't matter. I knew my passion would help me find a way. All I knew was that I didn't want any child or individual to go through the gruesome events that I'd experienced. Everyone deserves to be happy; it's a God-given right; and so, did we.

Today, over forty years later since making that promise in 1980, I can say with great pride, that I have fulfilled it in every way possible. However, I do realise there is still much more work to be done, and with the grace of God, I will continue to live my promise for as long as I remain on this Earth. This is only the beginning.

During the 1970s me and my brother Charanjit, faced a very tough childhood, and I mean tough. We lived on Rangal Road in Canning Town, East London. At that time, my family and I regularly met extraordinary levels of racism. Memories of the abuse we suffered are as clear to me today as if they had happened only yesterday. Due to these incidents, my family and I have had to find ways to deal with our very own mental health issues.

By the time I was thirteen, I could neither read nor write. My primary school years were overshadowed by relentless bullying and the deep-seated prejudice exhibited by some educators. For me, daily survival took precedence over academics. Amid these challenges, it was a struggle to focus on learning. So, taking that into consideration, completing this book fills me with pride, and I'm resolute in my belief that it's the first of many to come.

I began penning these memoirs in 2003, following the birth of our first child, Josh.

Embracing him, I was steadfast in my conviction that he would not endure the hardships of my youth. Britain has evolved; overt racism is less common, and numerous laws have fostered a climate of equality and diversity. While I recognise that Josh, like all of us, will face his own set of challenges, I remain hopeful that the cruel prejudice I encountered growing up as a young Asian Sikh boy in Canning Town will be foreign to him.

In the 1970s, to many prejudiced White-British individuals, our perceived transgression was merely our skin colour. Since then, the United Kingdom has grown more inclusive, embracing a tapestry of ethnicities. Yet, it's disheartening to acknowledge that some vestiges of racism still persist. Today's difference lies in society's reduced tolerance for blatant racism.

Throughout my childhood, I fervently recited a nightly prayer. Overwhelmed by fear and nestled under my blankets, I sought divine intervention, hoping those around me — school children, educators, and the White-British community — would see beyond my skin colour and faith. The era was marred by extremists, fuelled by a misguided ideology to 'Keep Britain White', shunning the idea of diverse ethnicities — be it African, Chinese, or others — integrating into the UK. Tragically, many among them were willing and did resort to using violence to further their cause.

Originally, my main motivation to write my childhood story was so that future generations of my family would fully appreciate and respect the lives that they are living, while not having faced the immense daily racist challenges that we did. By writing my story the intention was not to gain sympathy but to give encouragement and promote determination and fortitude in others who may be facing similar situations. To begin with, I never even thought about having this biography published.

In 2007, four years after the birth of Josh, our second child was born, our princess, Alisha. As the midwife passed this little angel to me, Alisha instantly wrapped her soft fingers around my index finger. I smiled, my heart filled, and uncontrollable tears of happiness flowed. No one was going to mistreat my children; they would live happy and prosperous lives, and enjoy their childhood, an experience that every child should live gracefully.

As soon as my children became old enough to understand, my wife Emma and I taught them the equality laws of the land. We disciplined them to practice fairness, speak the truth, respect other people's differences and always support people who needed their help. I wanted my children to follow my footsteps and support anti-bullying principles, and motivate the people around them.

I am so proud to say, they have. One day it will be their responsibility to teach the future generations the same virtues and values.

When I told my children, friends, and relatives about my turbulent childhood, they encouraged me to share the stories. Like many people do, I, too, could have locked these memories away somewhere in the deep recesses of my mind, never to be mentioned again. But I didn't. As I began to write, I realised that it wasn't easy to relive those disastrous days, and I still wasn't convinced that I should share them until Emma said something to me that made me click.

Her words were poetic, "Jag, you must tell the world your story. It clearly shows the true power of the human spirit. Your stories will surely, indefinitely, motivate and empower everyone who reads them…"

As I continue to write my childhood remembrances, I receive many compliments for having the courage to put pen to paper.

My duty and purpose in life is simple yet important: to encourage others to live their lives full of achievement and betterment. My wife made me realise that my memoirs could change lives and motivate others who were going through difficult times to stand up and challenge any unfair treatment they were experiencing.

If you, as a reader, can relate to what I went through and have a child who is suffering from being bullied, or if you are experiencing this in your workplace or relationship, please reach out and get help. This includes hate crime, mental health issues or lack of confidence. My advice to you is loud and clear: there are people out there who can and want to support you; speak to them immediately. Remember, you are not alone, and please, never, ever suffer in silence. To provide extra support, we have added a list of support groups at the end of this book. Unfortunately for me, I encountered all the above simultaneously: hate crime, mental health issues and lack of confidence. I will always remember the 'promise' I made to myself all those years ago. The 'promise' stands firm by my side and will forever remain 'Unbreakable.'

CHAPTER 1
THIS TOO SHALL PASS

ALMOST FIFTY YEARS AGO, MY BROTHER and I attended Sparrowfield Primary School, Canning Town, in East London. This story is based on those horrific days. At the time, we lived at No. 1 Rangal Road, a few blocks away from the school. This was our family's home between 1973 and 1980, when I was three to ten years old.

We were not horrible kids. Our parents taught us well, and we followed their values and beliefs of being polite, kind and friendly at all times. Just like any other child, all we wanted to do was to make good friends in school. This wasn't possible because of our differences. We were darker-skinned, unlike the other white children; we were of Indian descent with hair plaits tied at the back of our heads. As young Sikh males, this is the norm for our religion.

Basically, all the other children in our school were white, so everything about us, our hairstyle, skin colour, and mum's Indian cooking scent lingering on our clothes, all stood out. At that time if I had received a pound for each time the children or teachers at school had said: "Oi! You fuckin' stinker. You smell of 'orrible foreign Indian food!" I am confident that I would have become a wealthy man. Images of Sikh boys with hair plaits, a hair bobble or topknot and Sikh men wearing turbans or Pagri as known in Punjabi, were not a familiar sight in Britain at the time. For many White-

British residents, this was abnormal and unacceptable, unlike today. Having said that, there were occasional English folk who were intrigued by our hairstyle, who found our religion fascinating, and who would ask genuine questions. But unfortunately, they were a rarity, and it was more the opposite. It became clear to my brother and me, at a young age, that the majority of the White-British people where we lived hated us for who we were. Sometimes in life, you don't get a choice and just have to live with the cards you're dealt. We realised very early that we'd been dealt an appalling hand.

Being the only Asian boys in school opened the floodgates for the white bullies to target us daily. We might as well have had a 'KICK ME!' sign on our backs.

One bullying tactic which really got to me was the nasty, horrible and degrading act of spitting. The spitters were the bane of my life, and fifty years on, I can still vividly recall the whole disgusting, animal-like experience. Usually, it happened when I walked around school, minding my own business. Then, without warning or caution, some kids would approach me. I'd hear the oh so familiar sound of them drawing phlegm and saliva back into their throats to create a mucous ball. Once they had amassed sufficient volume and toxicity, they would let their concoction fly and launch their so-called masterpiece in my direction. The attack would happen so fast, unprovoked and within seconds: "...KHAAAA-TOOO!"

Instinctively, my hands would shoot up to cover my face. Invariably, they'd aim at my head, often my face and frequently my eyes. Whenever the bullies' slimy saliva hit my eyes, it stung like hell! I know it sounds terrible, but as the bullies were going to spit at me anyway, I would've preferred their nasty discharge to land anywhere else except the inside of my eyes. That's why I always dreaded the unexpected spitter. I could tolerate the punching, kicking and pushing that came from these bullies. Even being tripped over many times for no apparent reason, but the 'spit in the eye' was something I never got used to in those horrid school years.

Fortunately, today, the schools in East London and around the country are packed with diverse ethnic and multicultural children, which makes me so happy. But unfortunately for us, growing up in the seventies, in East London, this wasn't the case. We were in the wrong place and at the wrong time. We were pioneers in the introduction of multicultural ethnic groups to the UK. Looking back at that time, a part of me feels proud to be one of the first individuals to bring multiculturalism to Britain, but then I think about the gruesome negativity we endured, and any feelings of pride are instantly shattered.

Okay, so let's start from the top. Let me explain a little bit about our religious beliefs and my family's roots to help you understand the contrast between the residents of Canning Town and us at that time.

Khalsa is the name given to a community that considers Sikhism as their faith and religion. Khalsa was formed in 1669 by the last living Guru of Sikhism, Guru Gobind Singh. Since then, Singh is the surname given to all the male members of Sikhism and the Khalsa. It represents the warrior castes of Northern India. Although not all Singh's are blood-related, they carry this surname and represent a close-knit family unit. The Khalsa women members of the religion carry the surname Kaur rather than Singh, illustrating that they too are the female members of the Khalsa Sikh family. I am a Sikh, and I'm a Singh. I always have been, and always will be, proud of my religion.

My dad, Rajbans Singh, a proud turbaned Sikh, came to England as a first-generation immigrant from the Punjab, North India. In 1967, at only twenty-two years of age, this lanky and smart-looking young man left his family to have an arranged marriage with my mum Prabhjit Kaur. My dad's parents, Mr Kishan Singh Diraag, lovingly known as Papa Kishan by his children and grandchildren, and Mother, Mrs Gurcharan Kaur Diraag explained to Dad that England would be an attractive place for him to start a family.

Papa Kishan explained to my dad that the education system in the United Kingdom was the best in the world, the job prospects were high, and the strength of the pound sterling would always be strong due to the country's economic power. They all agreed that these factors would benefit my dad and the future generations of his family. My mum, a devout Sikh, was born in Delhi, India. Her family were also first-generation immigrants who arrived in England in 1950 when my mum was five.

My parents' firstborn son, my elder brother, Charanjit, was born in 1968, in the UK, a year after my parents' wedding. The UK family elders nicknamed Charanjit 'Bobby' because they all supported the West Ham United Football Club, and 'Bobby' Moore had captained the England football team to win the 1966 World Cup. It somehow seemed fitting. They hoped that, being the firstborn of a new generation, he would achieve equal success for his contemporaries, just as the legendary England football team captain had done.

Then, there was me, Jagjit Singh, born in 1970, I was their second child. Finally, our family was completed with our beloved baby sister Sharanjit Kaur, born in 1975. All three of us are native English, unlike our parents, who were born in India.

Our mother and dad have always been proud Sikhs and have remained fully committed to the traditions and beliefs of the Sikh religion. One fundamental tradition of Sikhism is the non-cutting of hair out of respect for the perfection of God's creation. This meant that Bob and I would follow in our dad's footsteps. First, as toddlers, we had our hair in plaits tied up at the back of our heads. As we got older, we tied our hair in a bobble on top of our heads like a top knot. Finally, we graduated to wearing a turban, completing the cycle, with full pride, as a visible sign of our commitment to our religion and ancestors.

In our school, we caused a great deal of curiosity due to our skin colour and religious hairstyles. The kids in our school often asked questions that would leave us embarrassed and humiliated like, "Why have you got long hair like a girl? Why don't you cut it? Are you a freak?" or "Why is your skin different? Is it because you haven't had a bath?" and "Do you come from Pakistan? Is that why they call you a Paki?"

In the beginning, we tried to explain that we weren't from Pakistan but from India. The explanation fell on deaf ears; it didn't change anything. We were still called Paki's. It seemed it was easier for the racists to put all light, brown-skinned Asian people in a single category; 'Paki's'. That was that. To me, this clearly illustrated the lack of education and stupidity of the white-racists of the nineteen-seventies. The teachers were just as bad when we tried to explain Sikhism to them; they laughed and humiliated us even more. Eventually, we gave up trying to explain.

Given that I was the youngest kid in my year and shorter in stature compared to the other children, this gave enough ammunition and plenty of reasons for the children and teachers to pick on me and hurl constant abuse at me. Bob, on the other hand, was very tall for his age, which gave him a slight advantage with the bullies. Some thought twice about attacking him due to his size, but it didn't count for anything when they ganged up on him. With different coloured skin, hair plaits, and being the smallest and youngest boy in my year, surrounded by racist teachers and children, I was doomed! I was taunted for many years due to these so-called highlighted 'abnormalities'.

I've never forgotten when I was with Mum in the local butchers on Barking Road. I was seven years old. In those days, you could only get fresh-cut ham, not packaged. I used to love watching the butcher slice the hind leg of pork so expertly with his sharp knife. On this particular day, an older white lady came waddling towards Mum and me. She bent down, looked me straight in the face and with a charming smile said, "Hot init' just like your country!"

I believe she thought she was genuinely being friendly, but her words confused me for months. What did she mean by 'just like your country '? As far as I was concerned, Britain was my country; I was born here. It took some time for me to realise she was talking about India. This was another example of British people displaying their ignorance. As far as they were concerned, we were classed as foreigners, even though I was born here. How could I be a foreigner?

It didn't stop there. The old lady then turned to my mum, pointed at me and said, "Isn't she a pretty girl?"

Me? Pretty girl? I was a boy with hair plaits! Why did everyone think I was a girl?

Mum politely corrected the old lady, "He is actually a boy."

"Oh?" The old woman was now intrigued. "Then why has he got hair plaits at the back of his head like a girl?'

Mum went on to explain about our religion. This wasn't the first, nor would it be the last time Mum would be asked this question, or me for that matter. I heard it every day, the difference being that the school kids weren't anywhere near as polite as the old lady and would call me names such as weirdo, freak, and many others. It was so embarrassing, I just wanted people to leave me alone, but that wasn't going to happen. There was no getting away from the abuse.

Our parents explained to us the ways of 'Sikhism' — truthful, helpful, bravery, modesty — the list would go on. The values gave us a mission to do good, and we accepted that. Both of our parents taught us well. Whenever we were out as a family, many white people would hurl abusive and racist remarks at us; Mum and Dad would tell us to ignore them. We tried, but it was hard as we were only young. It hurt our feelings, knowing that we couldn't even walk the streets without being sworn at or called a Paki. I mean, it was bad enough that we had to face this crap at school, let alone on the street as well.

We were brought up to be proud Sikhs. Our parents said we had to fully believe, or our prayers would go unheard. They tried to convince us that one day the people of Britain would accept Sikhs and other ethnic groups, and we would be left alone. Being only young and experiencing daily abuse, we didn't share their positive vision of the future.

I often spoke to God, although at times, I found it hard to believe that he really, truly existed. I never told my parents about my thoughts on God because they were way too religious and wouldn't understand, but I had my reasons. I struggled to believe in the power of prayer because of the many nights I spent crying, alone, begging, really begging for God to change things for me and to make the bullying stop. In bed, I would cover my face with my duvet and let the tears flow, discreetly, making sure that nobody heard. I didn't want to worry my family.

My brother Bob was always there for me; every time he caught me crying, he would try his best to comfort me.

"Why are you crying, Jag? What did I tell you about crying? It will only make them stronger."

I was always looking for answers, "Why do we get bullied every day, Bob? Yelled at by teachers even if we don't do anything wrong? And kicked about by the kids at school? Why?"

Bob would try his best to encourage me to have faith, but no matter what he said, I found it hard to see that this would ever end.

"Jag, one day it will all be okay, I promise. Just hang in there, little bro!"

One day?! Eventually? I wanted the change now! I wanted a happy life right now, just like any child should have!

I would frequently challenge Bob's words: "Yes, but Bob, that's only if we make it out of our childhood alive! I am only seven years old, Bob, and you are eight, and look at the crap we have to tolerate every day—it's getting worse!"

Bob never gave up hope, "Jag, you must do what Mum, Dad and the Sikh Gurus have told us to do, pray and pray more!"

"I don't really see the point of praying, Bob! I spend all night praying for a better life, but nothing ever changes; it's the same thing day in day out! If it isn't one bully, we can always rely on another bully waiting to hound us down! Why? Because we have different coloured skin and it's not white? God isn't real Bob; I am going to stop praying!"

During these conversations, Bob would always try his utter best to console me: "Jag, if you stop praying, there will be no hope. You must pray that one day things will get better. If you don't, then things won't change. And we need hope, or we are doomed forever." So, I carried on praying.

I felt my disbelief in God was justified by my surroundings, but Bob would still put on a brave face and encourage me to pray for the best. He would always remind me of the old Persian adage, which has been translated and used in multiple languages over the years: This too shall pass. Bob spoke many wise words of encouragement throughout our childhood, but the best statement he made to me frequently was: "Jag, we are here, at the wrong place, at the wrong time. And, if we can find a way to get through this and survive, then one day we will be at the right place, at the right time."

I'd regularly cried myself to sleep because I dreaded having to enter the tall school gates – the gates of hell – again, the next day. Whenever I walked to school, the closer I got, the sweatier my palms became, and my heart pumped like a steam engine gaining tremendous speed. There was no escape. Every day, I felt like a lamb to the slaughter, and I would begin to think about the diabolical bullying actions that awaited me. I'd look about with extreme suspicion and wonder which bully would attack me first, and even tried to guess which teacher would segregate and belittle me in front of the other children...again! It hurt, and I'd want to cry, but couldn't in front of the children and teachers. Instead, I'd save it for when I was alone, in bed. I stopped crying in front of other kids at a very early age, as it only encouraged further laughter and mockery.

CHAPTER 2
HARD GRAFT

23rd October 1965.

MY DAD AND HIS SIDE OF THE FAMILY come from the small village of Bundala in the Amritsar District, of Punjab, India, located close by the holy Sikh shrine, Darbar Sahib, also known as The Golden Temple. His dad, my granddad, Papa Kishan, was a highly educated man and Senior Clerk with the Magistrates Court in the Amritsar District Court. In his job, Papa Kishan mingled with many lawyers and judges and was considered to be a very knowledgeable person. So much so that he was frequently consulted whenever there were complicated cases.

Although Papa Kishan wasn't a tall man, less than five foot in height, nor broad in stature, he carried with him the strength and confidence of a lion. When he spoke or lost his temper, it was guaranteed that everyone would hear his deafening roar. Papa Kishan was a respected man.

In his late teens, my dad didn't enjoy studying, so Papa Kishan gave him the options of either applying himself to get a place at an Indian university or getting married and settling down. Dad jumped at the latter and agreed to an arranged marriage in England. He definitely didn't want to study; instead, he wanted to settle down and have his own family. Papa Kishan was a very stern and ambitious individual who was always open to advancement and self-development. He knew sending his son to England was definitely a form of improvement for the family. Additionally, my dad would be the first person in his whole entire family to migrate to England, to a western country.

The news spread throughout the village that Dad was going to travel to England by aeroplane, and everyone became extremely concerned. That's because they all strongly believed that flying objects in the sky were some forms of black magic and would eventually crash to the ground. The ensuing uproar amongst many of his friends and family petrified Dad. Even though he was in his twentieth year, he eventually convinced himself that flying to England to marry my mum was a death sentence!

Of course, Papa Kishan knew differently, and over time, Dad met many people who had actually flown to England and survived. These individuals attempted to reassure him that there was nothing to worry about, and in fact, that England, or more precisely, London, the so-called 'City of Dreams', was a place full of opportunities. He was told that there were plenty of jobs for hard workers, and if he saved up enough money, it wouldn't be long before he could buy his own house. They explained to Dad that England would serve his children with the best education they could have. Despite all these promises, the negative voices of the villagers caused him continued doubt. But he was adamant that he didn't want to go to university, so Dad decided to take a risk and prayed that his aeroplane wouldn't fall out of the sky.

The day of his departure arrived. Thirty-seven

villagers, all family and friends, went to see him off at the Indira Gandhi International Airport, Delhi. He was petrified as he waited to board the plane. It didn't help that all the family and friends were there not to wish him good luck, but to mourn his death and tell him he was going to die! Only Papa Kishan comforted him and told him not to pay any attention.

Dressed in his best tailor-made suit—a gift from Papa Kishan for the special occasion—my dad bravely smiled at his dad at the airport, as he tried his best to hide his fears.

Before he finally departed, my dad's parents passed him an overcoat. He was told he would need to wear it when he arrived in the U.K. since the weather was always cold, even in the summer. Many male immigrants who immigrated to England always dressed professionally for their plane journey. It wasn't only the Indian foreigners who came to England who wore a suit and an overcoat. The Africans, Muslims, and Chinese all did the same. They represented their country and did so with their professional dress sense and pride as they headed towards England, the prestigious land ruled by the Queen. Overcoats were always necessary, as they had all been warned about the cold British weather.

My dad finally hugged Papa Kishan, and both had their eyes filled with tears. Then, Dad turned and almost wailed as he fell into his mother's arms. They both felt it was the last time they would ever see each other. Their feelings were justified and correct. This was the last time they would meet and see each other. Never again. My dad's mother (my grandmother),

Gurcharan Kaur, would eventually lose her battle with her diabetes. She passed away well before my dad could save up enough money and afford to go to visit her in India. Although my dad left behind two brothers and two sisters in India when he came to England, his mother never ever truly got over the sadness of losing a child who went far away to live in a foreign country. She missed him dearly.

Whenever my dad recalled this journey from India to England, he always said it was the scariest flight he had ever made. Dad prayed continuously throughout the trip, softly mumbling prayers and sweating as he held on to the armrests for dear life. Unknowingly, he kept nudging the passengers on either side of him, expecting the plane to fall out of the sky at any moment. It didn't happen, of course. After Dad landed, he sent a telegram back to Bundala Village announcing he'd arrived safely. The villagers celebrated and thanked God for the miracle that had taken place.

My dad had a limited education and spoke only broken English when he arrived in England. He had a very restricted vocabulary. As the years passed, my mum and her brothers and sister supported my dad and helped him improve his English. It would take him many years of practice before he spoke fluent English and finally mastered the Cockney rhyming slang. His lack of fluency and Western education meant that the type of jobs he could apply for was restricted. But what he lacked in ability, he made up for in enthusiasm and hard work.

At that time, he was looking for work in Stratford, East London. There was a particular building housing many factory units close to the shopping centre. The factory building was surrounded by derelict land and was nothing like the shiny upcoming Metropolitan area today.

My dad's search for work was relentless. He woke up at nine every morning, washed and put on one of the grand suits that he'd acquired as wedding gifts. Then, with great thought, he'd find a splendid matching tie. Finally, he would top off his ensemble with a proudly worn turban. Once he looked smart and felt confident, his dad-in-law, my mum's dad, Mr Mahindar Singh Tooray, would drive him to Stratford and drop him off outside the factory building. Here he would begin his cold-calling journey. Each day, without an appointment, he'd go systematically from factory to factory asking for work.

At that time, each of these factories was occupied by White-British employers. Knocking on the doors or ringing the doorbells frequently meant waiting for ages before someone answered. And when they did, many of the employers would give my dad a puzzled look. Before them, they saw this slim, smartly dressed Indian man standing at their door, wearing a turban and speaking in broken English.

"My name is Raj; I am looking for work...I am a hard worker..."

His success rate was dismal, to say the least. Some employers let Dad down politely, but the majority would laugh at him, ridiculing his speech with mocking imitations. They would eventually slam their door in his face if they had even bothered to open it in the first place. Others were far more direct, "We don't employ Paki's or darkies! Now fuck off!"

The first time this happened, he almost broke down into tears. He was shocked at the hostile response, which he hadn't expected. He'd always been a religious, peaceful and loving person who never reacted to any obscene behaviour made towards him. He didn't have an ounce of rudeness within him; all he wanted was a job. Dad absolutely hated being sworn at and felt humiliated. But he needed a job, so he bravely continued his quest, eventually becoming immune to such behaviour since he didn't have much choice.

He maintained this daily routine for almost a month. With no luck, he became despondent and decided to give up, realising that his approach wasn't working. He felt disheartened, sad, and like a total failure; he'd left his family behind in India to come to England with a plan to get married, find a job, and live happily ever after in 'The City of Dreams', London. The reality was he just couldn't find a job! It took some time before he understood that it wasn't him per se, but rather, he'd come to England during a time when a potent cloud of racism hung over the country. The racism was fuelled by the media, especially TV, which created hatred within many of the white residents towards Indians, Blacks, and other ethnic minorities: they were all public enemy number one! It was a matter of terrible timing for my poor ole' Dad.

No one wanted to employ Dad. All he wanted was a job he could work hard at and then settle down, have children, and eventually buy a house. But he was stuck at the first hurdle, struggling to find a job. Although he highly appreciated the support of my mum's parents, Mr Mahindar Singh and his wife, Mrs Kailash Kaur, for letting him and Mum stay in their house until Dad got a job and a place of his own, Dad desperately wanted to be independent and stand on his own two feet.

♦♦♦

16th June 1967.
This day was pivotal for my dad in achieving a significant part of his life plan — securing a job. Having knocked on fifteen factory units and getting fifteen rejections plus a considerable amount of abuse, he felt tired, hopeless and discouraged. He stormed out of the building, took a deep breath, and looked up at the cloudy, overcast sky before praying to God for support and strength.

"Dear Waheguru (Punjabi word used in Sikhism to refer to God. Wahi means 'Wonderful', and Guru is a term denoting 'Teacher'), please help me find a job. That's all I want, right now! Please show me the way."

As soon as he finished praying, my dad remembered Papa Kishan's words of wisdom: 'Whenever you are faced with any challenge, keep calm, pray and never, ever give up.'

At that thought, he shook his head and brushed off the negativity. With a renewed sense of purpose, he stopped the self-pity and decided to give the job hunting another try. He marched back into the factory building and continued knocking on the doors, but sadly, still met with the same rejections and worse. Many factories would peek through their door spy holes, and once they saw Dad standing outside, they would intentionally ignore him.

By late afternoon, drained and thoroughly disillusioned, he strolled over to a telephone box and called his dad-in-law to ask him if he'd be so kind as to come and pick him up. While he waited, Dad slumped onto a nearby bench in utter despair. Looking about, he noticed a white van parked directly outside the factory units building. As he watched, two men, talking in strong Irish accents, unloaded some boxes out of the van. They shifted the load inside the building to factory unit number 35. Dad knew from his earlier endeavours that this unit had been unoccupied. He sprang to his feet and sprinted to the van just as the men reappeared. Without hesitation, he introduced himself, "Hello gentlemen, my name is Raj Singh...I am looking for work...I am a hard worker."

One of the men, a short, stubby man with a broad smile, responded, "Hey, I've heard about you guys! All you Indian Sikhs are hard grafters!"

Dad struggled to understand the accent; the only word he had recognised was Sikh's. It sounded promising, but Dad still didn't get his hopes up. "Yes, sir, I am looking for a job?"

"Job? You want a job, Mr Singh?"

"Yes...Please...You can call me Raj."

The man reached out and offered him a welcoming handshake. "Hi, I'm Kieran O'Sullivan. I own a pram factory. Would you like to work for me?"

Dad had only a rough idea of what Kieran had just said.

"What was that, sir?" Dad needed Kieran to explain again. Kieran realised that Dad was struggling with his accent and began to speak slowly.

"You...can...work...for me."

"Work for you? Yes, sir, please!" At the offer of work, Dad was so happy that his legs began to wobble with excitement, he felt light-headed and thought he was about to faint

Kieran could clearly see the excitement in his eyes. "Okay, Mr Singh, please report to work tomorrow at 9am. We make prams and need help with our production. And, although I love the suit, you can wear casual clothes. We won't mind."

It took some time, but as the months passed, Dad eventually began to tune in to Kieran's Irish accent.

Persistence paid off. My dad proudly delivered the good news to the family and thanked everyone for their support. That evening, he wrote a letter to his parents in India and shared the fantastic news, purposely failing to mention the struggles and racism he'd endured in his job search, believing they didn't need to know.

The next day, Dad turned up at factory number 35 at 08:30 precisely, well ahead of the required time. Kieran invited him in; Dad noticed three other turbaned Sikhs fixing handles onto prams. Among these Sikh

workers, he also saw four white men speaking with Irish accents.

This was the first time Dad met Bhupinder, who would later become his best friend. Although unrelated, we always called him 'Uncle' because he and Dad eventually developed a great relationship, just like true brothers. They had so much in common. Both were in their twenties and from the Punjab. They had both come to England for an arranged marriage and both struggled with the English language.

One old white-haired Irish worker put his thumb up at Dad, "Welcome to K.P.F.' Kieran's Pram Factory', Mr Singh! I am Liam!"

One by one, all the workers got up, gave Dad a comfortable handshake, and introduced themselves. He couldn't believe it; he had actually found a job, and his soon-to-be work colleagues all appeared to be very friendly.

After all the staff had acquainted themselves, Kieran walked into the assembly area, smiled and placed his arm behind my dad's back, "Oh, good! You've all met Raj. He's joining our team and will be working on the Wheels Machine." Kieran looked in Dad's direction. "The job's a bit repetitive, boring..."

Dad showed Kieran his appreciation. "Sir, I have been knocking on the doors of the factories for a long time. I will do whatever work you would like me to do, sir... I am hard worker. Thank you, sir."

♦♦♦

Dad spent many enjoyable years at the pram factory

and felt Kieran O'Sullivan was one of the best bosses he'd ever had. They all became good friends. During their lunch breaks, they would share and swap their homemade Irish and Indian dishes. The Irish workers would bring in their delicious Irish soups and stews, and the Sikh workers took turns bringing in onion bhajis, samosas, and authentic curries. Lunchtime was always a fabulous and enjoyable feast for them all.

My dad and his Indian colleagues would always take their work lunch in a metal 'Tiffen' box, a classic Indian three-tier food container. The tiffin not only kept the food warm but was also compact and easy to carry. Many Indian wives around the world, including my mum, would fill their husbands' tiffins' two compartments with Indian curries and the third section with Chapattis. This traditional food container is still used throughout the world, especially in India.

On special occasions such as Diwali and St. Patrick's Day, Kieran would take his hospitality towards his workers a step further. He would supply a cheeky glass or two of Whiskey for his staff after work. He loved his workforce. They were all elite in their allocated jobs, and Kieran called them all 'hard grafters' daily. Dad told me that it was a fun place to work. The quality controller at the factory, who checked the work, was always amazed by their efficiency and hard work. While assembling the prams, the workers would take turns singing Sikh and Irish folk songs throughout the day, keeping their spirits high.

The factory had a great working atmosphere, considering the racism and prejudices they faced outside the premises. Just like the Sikhs, Muslims and other ethnic groups, the Irish also faced the same daily racist challenges. Every one of the workers had met with difficulties similar to Dad's when searching for work. So, no one complained about anything and just appreciated the fact that they had a job. Dad believed he would never have got work if Kieran had been British and always thanked Kieran for allowing him to prove himself.

The wages at the pram factory were meagre, in fact, lower than the average pay at the time, but it was all Kieran could afford. There were no perks, and the factory itself was too small for the workers to move around adequately, given the number of pram parts that were left lying around.

As the years progressed, Kieran's pram business boomed. Dad worked all the overtime that came his way and eventually saved enough money for a rental deposit. He and Mum moved into a one-bedroom flat in Bengal House, Whitechapel, East London. After a year, my mum gave birth to my elder brother Bob, and two years later, I was born in 1970. The flat felt massive, with plenty of space for two growing children. Whitechapel was becoming a highly Asian populated area. Dad and Mum felt safe there, away from the racist cowards, and so did others. Within a few months, my dad passed his driving test and bought his first car, a Hillman Hunter Estate. Things were looking up. Finally, everything began falling into place, and Mum and Dad were over the moon.

Early in September 1971, Kieran decided to move back to Ireland and run the business from there.

The costs of operating from London were high, with the annual factory rent increasing at a fast pace. This was unfortunate for Dad and his colleagues. Dad had aspirations of buying a house and saved monthly, but he still didn't have enough, and now he was out of work. Undeterred, Dad started his search for work immediately, even returning to knocking on the factory doors again. With no success, he had no choice but to use all his savings for daily living expenses. Before he knew it, Dad was back to square one - no job and no deposit to purchase a house; he went back to the drawing board.

♦♦♦

Some six months passed before Dad's good friend Bhupinder told him about a newly opened glass factory in Silvertown, which was looking for workers. Both Dad and Bhupinder applied, and as the word spread, so did many other ethnic groups. Dad and Bhupinder were successful, and for the first time in his life, Dad found himself working for an English employer. He couldn't believe it. He had a clocking card, an on-site canteen and a uniform! Dad was flattered by the great opportunity he had been given to work in a major factory plant. All the ethnic groups that worked there thought themselves lucky. Dad's whole family was so proud of him in England and India. And for Dad and Mum, it was like a dream come true: he was back on track, saving for a mortgage deposit.

The glass factory had a very different working environment from that of the pram factory. With a workforce of around three hundred and only a handful of ethnicities, it was predominantly a white, British environment. The Black, Indian, Muslim, and Irish workers kept themselves to themselves, becoming a close-knit community. They enjoyed each other's company in the work canteen and even met up in the local pub for a few games of darts on the weekends or after work.

Racism proliferated and spread within the workplace as well. Both the glass factory's managers and workers ridiculed the Sikhs, laughed at their turbans and took the Mickey out of their broken English accents. Rather than calling ethnics by their names, they tormented them by using all sorts of humiliating terms like Darkies, Nig-Nogs and Paki's. The managers were no better and would allocate the ethnic employees the nastiest, most horrid cleaning jobs. At the same time, the white workers got all the best tasks, such as operating the machines.

My dad and his colleagues found the situation very offensive but kept quiet. Instead of resisting, they tolerated these behaviours. Eventually, they came to accept them as the norm to the extent that they saw themselves as second-class citizens and simply appreciated the fact that they were lucky enough to have jobs, no matter how menial they were! Dad and Uncle Bhupinder dearly missed Kieran, and they would regularly reminisce about those wonderful days working at the pram factory.

As Dad and his ethnic friends had already learned through their personal experiences, it was hard to get a job if you weren't white and British, especially if you didn't speak English reasonably well. Like Dad, many of his ethnic friends struggled with the language. At that time, the white employer and employee were much more dominant and influential than first-generation immigrant workers. No workplace equality was practised, as equal opportunities were not compulsory by law. This was so unfortunate for my dad and his colleagues. It was a case of keeping a brave face and never telling their families about the daily abuse. They tolerated the mistreatment with their heads down and feared standing up for themselves. They couldn't chance losing their jobs as they had families to support; instead, they kept quiet and endured the racist behaviours.

Dad worked all the possible hours, including fifteen-hour shifts, and finally saved enough money for a mortgage deposit. He was now ready to become a homeowner. Bob and I were growing up fast, and we needed more space since the flat was packed with toys, bikes and clothes. Plus, Dad hated paying rent at the flat in Bengal House. He always said, "Paying rent was like throwing your hard-earned money away in the river. Money paid towards rented accommodation never comes back. Once it's gone, it's gone forever."

CHAPTER 3
CANNING TOWN

17th March 1973.

DAD, EXCITED BY THE PROPOSITION of buying a house sought advice. In those days, there was no internet for researching where the best areas were; instead, people relied on word of mouth. The only words of caution from my uncles and aunts were to avoid the Woolwich area. At the time Woolwich was highly dominated by 'Skinheads'; a lethal racist gang, with a heightened hatred for Indians, Blacks and other ethnics. Given the notorious reputation, no ethnic individuals would walk or drive through Woolwich. The rumours were, that if you dared to, you'd never come back out alive! Many stories were told of skinheads verbally and physically abusing ethnics just for entertainment.

My parents were so excited when they visited the local Estate Agent on Barking Road. They were shown a folder of pictures of a substantially sized house on Rangal Road, Canning Town. Instantly, they both fell in love with the property and began to visualise their young children growing up harmoniously in this house. I was three years old at the time, and Mum had plonked me onto her ever-rocking knee. I was playing with my favourite Scooby-doo car, riding it up and down my leg, and wasn't really paying much attention to the conversation.

Four-year-old Bob was sitting on a separate chair next to Dad. He swung his legs back and forth with his mouth wide open, staring at the psychedelic white diamonds on the estate agent's massive 'kipper' tie, considered the height of fashion. At the same time, the agent kept looking at Bob's and my hair plaits while Mum and Dad scanned through the pictures of the property. Although he knew we were boys, he couldn't understand why we had hair plaits. I believe the agent had many questions but held back, for fear of offending my parents and potentially losing the sale.

Dad often struggled with the estate agents' patter, while mother, on the other hand, was a natural in speaking English and Cockney, having worked in numerous market stalls over the years. When dad couldn't understand, he'd squint, cut into the conversation, and look to mother for her to explain in Punjabi. What Bob and I found most fascinating was when the agent spoke directly to Dad; he spoke slowly, and with each word, he got louder. "It…is…a…very…good…house…Mr Singh. The area…location…is amazing!"

I know Dad struggled to understand the language, but it didn't mean he was deaf!

The estate agent rubbed his hands, taking turns looking at my mother and dad. His eyes widened, synchronising with his smile. "Canning Town is an up-and-coming area. The people are great, and the houses are massive, as you can see in the pictures. A quiet, peaceful area surrounds Rangal Road."

Mum and Dad had already fallen in love with

the property. In their mind, the sale was made, but the estate agent wasn't aware of this fact and continued his pitch,

"This house would be ideal for a young family just like yours, Mr and Mrs Singh. When are you looking to view the property? Would you like to see it right now? I have no appointments for the next hour. I can take you there myself."

Soon, in a procession, we followed the agent's light blue Morris Marina and headed for Rangal Road. On route, my parents saw that a local nursery and primary school were only a stone's throw away from our house, as well as a doctor's surgery and ample shops. As Dad turned the car into Rangal Road, both my parents looked at each other and beamed: there it was, No 1 Rangal Road. Their hearts leapt—they loved the property!

♦♦♦

We moved into our new home in April 1973. The estate agent was so right when he said the house was massive! Unlike the flat in Bengal House, we now had stairs and rooms upstairs. We were going to miss the old place, but we definitely appreciated the extra space, including a garden. Now, we actually have a garden of our own and no longer have to share a communal park with other residents, like we did in Bengal House. It was like a dream come true.

Inside our new house, on the ground floor, we had the main living room, and to the left, a kitchen from which we could access the garden. On the right-hand side of the living room was a room used as a bedroom. During the daytime, Bob and I would sit in this room, on our parents' bed, for ages. We'd dangle our little legs off their bed while we looked out of the front window through the netting, watching the world go by. We found it fascinating that we could see people, yet they couldn't see us. The old flat had been on the second floor, so we always looked down onto the heads of passers-by, but now we had a front-row view. We'd discuss where we thought the people were coming from, going to, or what their business was. At the time, we had no idea that this window would one day make our lives a living hell.

Upstairs were two enormous bedrooms, a small box room, and a bathroom. Dad planned to decorate the two spacious rooms for Bob and me, and as Mum and Dad knew they wanted a third child, he'd leave decorating the box room to some later time. None of this happened during our stay at Rangal Road; these plans never materialised. In fact, the bedrooms upstairs were never used, as there were many other pressing issues to deal with.

Mum and Dad slept in the ground-floor bedroom, while Bob and I each grabbed one of the two comfy sofas in the living room. These sofas became our beds; our living room was also our bedroom.

A couple of years after moving, my baby sister, Sharanjeet Kaur, was born in 1975. Our relatives in India and England were so proud of my dad's accomplishments in such a short time. He now had a good job, house, car and an upcoming young family. He had kept himself focused, worked hard and finally achieved his goal of becoming a British homeowner.

When mother and dad purchased our house, their intentions were simple: to see their children grow up living in peace and harmony. In the beginning, this house was like heaven, but little did I know that one day I would watch helplessly as it burned to the ground in front of my very own eyes.

CHAPTER 4
RULE, BRITANNIA!

24th January 1975.

BY THE MID-1970s England and the whole United Kingdom had been through two massive social and economic changes following the end of World War II. In the first, post-war Britain had to rebuild itself after the devastation of the German bombing raids; many of the returning soldiers felt displaced or were traumatised, and good quality housing was in short supply. On the positive side, the mass-production techniques developed during the 1940s to meet the insatiable demands of a country at war were turned into the production of household goods like TVs, radios, fridges and other consumer goods. A baby boom followed, causing a surge in population and pressure on health and social services. Also, the pre-war conservative attitudes were lost – people were freer to express themselves. Macmillan described the era, the Prime Minister of the day, as one in which "we've never had it so good."

The demand for workers outstripped the available supply. The government actively encouraged British citizens from the Caribbean (the Windrush Generation), the recently partitioned India and Pakistan, and Ireland to come to England to satisfy the demands. Given the booming economy and the belief that the streets were paved with gold, many colonial and Commonwealth nationals took up the offer.

Throughout the 1950s and 1960s, the influx of immigrants was less of an issue with the British population; the economy went from strength to strength. But come the seventies, when the economic boom turned sour, inflation hit 25%, oil prices soared, and unemployment followed, it was a very different story. If in the late 1950s, we'd never had it so good, by the mid-1970s, it seemed we'd never had it so bad. It was a return to the 1940s austerity with no obvious enemy, and the public were far less forgiving of this inconvenience as our family were about to find out.

Archibald 'Henry' Skipper slowly stroked his freshly shaved head using alternate hands. He preferred to be known as Archie and hated Archibald because his dad had always used his full name to bark at him as a child.

"Archibald! You're a little piece of shit! Get your arse here right now!"

Hearing his drunken dad shout, Archie knew what followed next would be an unjustified beating. That was a long time ago; today, at the age of twenty-five, Archie was proud that he had finally dealt with his alcoholic dad once and for all, freeing himself from his dad's devastating physical clutches. However, despite his freedom, Archie realised the memories of those beatings would be harder to escape.

In the small office space within the Woolwich Glow-lite car MOT centre, sitting on an old, creaky wooden chair, Archie leaned forward and dropped his head toward the floor. His head rubbing revealed the matching swastika tattoos inked on either side of his temples, gained during his time in Chelmsford Prison. Archie had demanded that a tattooist inmate apply the symbols so everyone he met would know precisely what he stood for.

'General Archie' had chosen the Glow-lite MOT centre for tonight's gathering as the guy who owned the place shared Archie's vision and wanted to support the cause. Although Archie had only been sitting for a few minutes, it seemed an eternity to him. His head rubbing sped up as he felt hot and nauseous. Sweat beaded on his forehead, gradually trickling down until it began to drip off the tip of his nose. The confined office space brought back the claustrophobic feeling he'd experienced in his prison cell. As usual, he took several deep breaths to break the pattern and focus his attention on his plans, vision and upcoming speech.

He was eager to unleash his message to his people so he could escape this untidy, hateful place as soon as possible. His speech was well prepared. All he had to do was deliver it with the same intensity and passion he felt for his beloved country.

Archie's two lieutenants came barging into the small office dressed similarly to him: bald heads, white vests, braces, jeans, and Dr. Marten's steel-toe-capped boots (DM's). This was the trademark fashion of the 'Skinheads'. The name of this ruthless group invoked fear then, as its memory still does for many today.

Robert Marsh, a mammoth-sized individual and Archie's first appointed Lieutenant, was the first through the office door. "They're ready for you, General Archie! They're ready to hear what you 'ave to say."

On delivering his message, Rob continuously punched his massive arms into the air while clenching his brick-sized fists. Floods of adrenaline and excitement rushed through his body. Archie shot up from his chair like a bullet, grabbed his right wrist and began to flex his massive bicep. He was showing off the well-built guns he had created courtesy of the HM prison's gym. The veins on his muscular shoulders and arms gradually got thicker and more prominent. Archie kept his head down and eyes on his arms as he whispered a response to his Lieutenant, "Yeah... I 'ope so, Lieutenant Robbie... I bloody well 'ope they're ready... they fuckin' need to be!" Even in a whisper, his venomous rhetoric came storming through his voice.

The Second Lieutenant was Tommy Gatsby, a humongous man with a massive anchor tattoo on his bulging right forearm. He strolled through the door with a smile hanging off his scar-decorated face, each one a trophy denoting some brutal act. Tommy expanded his broad chest and pointed towards the door, inviting his General to go and lead the gathering of devoted skinhead followers waiting impatiently.

The main workshop area of the MOT centre had been cleared of all cars to make room for the mob. The walls were specially decorated for the evening with banners bearing pictures of Hitler and plastered with Swastikas. The owner was okay with this, provided they were taken down by morning, as they weren't good for business: in the end, money triumphs.

There must have been at least thirty-five White-British youth all packed into the area being bathed in loud, heavy, head-banging music. The crowd of both men and women, swigged on cans of beer while they chuffed away on their fags one after another. The atmosphere was thick with smoke that easily swam around the place, and the din of many voices competing with the tribal-like music was constant.

Suddenly, the office doors leading to the workshop swung open. The music came to an abrupt halt, replaced by utter silence; you could have heard the proverbial pin drop. First, the two muscular skinhead lieutenants strolled in and stood on either side of the doorway; their arms folded and faces motionless. Within seconds, between the two massive lieutenants, their General, Archie Skipper, though not as tall but broader in bulk, barged through the doors and into the crowd-filled workshop. He marched forward toward a makeshift stage which had been set up for him. He would make his grand speech standing on a large stainless-steel workbench. The skinheads parted to let Archie through, careful not to bump into the General, not even accidentally, as they were all well aware it wouldn't have ended well.

As Robbie and Tommy marched behind their leader, they scanned each skinhead with their squinted eyes and vexed expressions, asserting power and dominance. The only sound was the thumping steps coming from the DMs of all three men as they headed toward the small stage.

Once he arrived at the workbench, Archie sprang onto it with acrobatic ease, flaunting his impressive physicality. He stood up straight facing the wall against the direction of his audience. Through his vest, he revealed his large traps, lats and multitude of muscles. His devoted lieutenants took up their positions on either side of him facing the crowd. Archie stood higher than anyone else, he squinted and grinned with pride at the wall poster of his mentor the Fuhrer of Nazi Germany, Adolf Hitler.

Without facing his crowd, he placed his hands on his hips and began his monologue, "It's great to see you all here! It's good to know that we still have some good ole' British beliefs floating about in our country... beliefs such as... keeping our country WHITE!! We need to burn the fuckin' Paki's and blacks, the whole fuckin' lot of them! White Supremacy rules!" Archie's hatred made him snarl like a rabid dog and spray spit as he spoke. He couldn't help letting his passion get the better of him.

Some of the skinheads cheered Archie on, "YEAH! YEAH!"

Others were shocked by his racist comments. Some felt uncomfortable as they were only now finding out what the gathering was about and regretted their attendance.

"As your appointed General, I am telling you that our work has only just begun. I have been speaking to the other skinhead generals based around London, and they are supporting and standing tall with us as brothers. They too share our ultimate goal and plan to scare the Paki's, Niggers, Chinkies and any other foreign fuckin' cockroaches out of our country! They are silently invading our territory...right in front of our very own fuckin' eyes!"

Archie finally took his gaze off the Hitler poster and turned to face his audience. The skinheads saw the rage in his bulging red eyes.

"Even if it means we shed their fuckin' blood...so fuckin' be it!" He slapped his fist to his chest before raising his arm into a Nazi salute. Many of the devoted skinheads followed suit.

A small group of skinheads were startled by Archie's outrageous comments and actions and shook their heads in disgust. These guys enjoyed the skinhead fashion scene and culture, but didn't want to see anyone hurt. The non-believers headed towards the exit. They hadn't signed up for this and didn't want to be part of it. Archie now shook his head in disbelief and disgust. For him, they were cowards and not worthy. They left one by one.

Archie intentionally directed his words at the departing skinheads.

"If you ain't got the bottle to be part of this legacy, this war, then get the fuck out of my sight. Right now! That's right, leave! I know each and every one of you, so if you speak to anyone about this gathering, I swear I'll fuckin' find you and skin you bastards alive!"

The handful of skinheads slowly departed from the MOT centre.

Archie cleared his throat, producing a slimy ball of phlegm, which he launched in their direction to show his disgust. "KHATOOT! Now fuck off you scum! Call yourself British? Get out of 'ere before I cut your bloody fuckin' throats!"

Some twenty or so devoted skinheads were now left inside the MOT centre. Archie nodded to Lieutenant Tommy Gatsby, who strolled over to the exit doors. Tommy understood Archie's wordless instructions and slammed the doors shut before nodding back to his General to continue with the gathering. Rob Marsh disappeared to the rear of the workshop, to return within seconds pushing a shopping trolley overflowing with beer cans. The two Lieutenants then started distributing the cans of Special Brew beer to the comrades who'd demonstrated their loyalty and stayed on. Lieutenant Tommy threw a can in Archie's direction.

After catching it in mid-air, Archie immediately flicked it open. "See! This is how we treat our people, drink up my friends..." He gulped half of the can within seconds.

The crowd chanted "Archie, Archie, Archie," as they all popped open their cans. One skinhead screamed out from the audience, "Thanks, Archie, for the Specials!" showing his appreciation for the beer. Archie laughed, "Oh, don't thank me! Thank the stupid Paki shop we robbed earlier. First, we walked into the local SPAR shop and nicked a fuckin' trolley. The woman at the counter said that she was going to call the police. I told her to shut the fuck up. Then, we strolled over to that Paki shop on Barking Road, near the Post Office. We walked in and right in front of their very own eyes we took six crates of beer, and the stupid Paki bastards couldn't say a word. They were so fuckin' petrified of us. They couldn't stop us! They didn't fuckin' dare!"

Archie raised his eyebrow, smiled and continued his speech as he watched his audience swig down their beer. "There's a reason why I, Archie

Skipper, 'ave been appointed your General and why my excellent lieutenants 'ave gained their positions. We've proven ourselves, earned our respect and served time in prison. We are proud of what we've done and what we stand for. After all, those foreign bastards we bled, bashed and sent to hospital needed to learn a fuckin' lesson or two. If the ole' bill hadn't turned up when they did, we'd have killed the fuckers! Now that me and my men 'ave shown our dedication to the cause through our actions, we've been chosen to lead this mission on our turf!"

"Archie! Archie! Archie!" The convinced crowd continued to show their support for their leader.

Robbie and Tommy exchanged glances and broadened their grins, knowing that the gathering was going exactly as the General had planned.

Archie spoke faster and more aggressively as the effects of alcohol kicked in. "Me and my colleague generals who are spread all over London, have plans, and we want you all to be a part of them. Plans to expand our revolution, our people and dominate this country as its rightful owners. How dare those bastards come from the fuckin' jungles and expect to live in our country! The fuckin' audacity! They can fuck right off!"

Swigging back their beers and dragging on their fags the crowd showed their agreement, "Yeeeah! Yeeeah!"

Buoyed up by the drunken crowd, Archie maintained the onslaught, "Our goal and purpose is to scare these ethnic bastards out of our country…I repeat…OUT OF OUR COUNTRY!"

Archie slugged back the remainder of his drink and threw the empty can at a nearby wall. Robbie tossed him another full can instantly on the basis that all this talking must be making the General thirsty. Archie flung his head back and chugged the whole can within a few seconds. Then, he crushed the can in his hand and tossed it onto the floor.

As he spoke, Archie gritted his teeth with rage, "Another Paki dared to open up a sweet shop on Barking Road right opposite Rangal Road. Bad move in our territory." He took turns in looking at his lieutenants as he grinned sadistically, "But our boys did a good number on him and chased him and his family out of town, once and for all, back to whatever fuckin' jungle he and his fuckin' family came from!"

All the spectators knew exactly what Archie's boys must have done to scare the family off.

Archie continued, "Once the Paki's had left, we moved in and made it our den. Ya' know, for us. The estate agent bloke came around and gave us some 'blah-blah police', 'blah-blah court', 'get out of the shop', 'vacate the premises', but we told him to fuck off, and if he didn't leave us alone, we would hunt down his family and cause them havoc and pain." Archie laughed hysterically, "I don't think he had much of a choice. He agreed and left!"

Archie stood up straight with dominance as he spoke, "We, the skinheads are ruling the country and need to expand, you know, spread our wings. So, we will use these newfound premises, this ex-sweet shop in Canning Town as our head office. Our main den. Make it our home. Then, we can have two territories,

Woolwich and Canning Town and later we'll 'ave three, then four and so on. In this new den, we will make plans, you know, to hunt out them foreigners who surround Barking Road. Attack more Indians, continue with the Paki-bashing, smash the Black Wogs and Chinkies...create fear, hunt them down! We are goin' to fuckin' war!"

The brain-washed crowd yelled out in excitement, "YEEAAGH!"

Archie's rant continued, "Our backup forces will remain in Woolwich, and I will take a few men, and we'll start to settle in Canning Town. I wanna make this new den the biggest skinhead location in the United Kingdom. And, from there we will attack, destroy their families, smash their windows and hurt their children until...they leave our fuckin' country. We will give their children fuckin' nightmares so that they fear us every time they go to bed! Also, I have many good friends in powerful positions who will support us if needs be. I know people in high places. If we can plant fear in these fuckin' immigrants, they will leave. If they don't, then they will have no choice but to face the wrath of The National Front! ARE...YOU...WITH ME?"

One by one, the skinheads in the room joined in and started to chant, "Archie! Archie! Archie!"

The General jumped down from the makeshift stage as he continued, "I've also heard that a few silly little vigilante groups are forming, you know Paki's, Darkies and them lot. Fuckin' wannabe heroes. But they 'aven't got a chance with us lot. Apparently, they are going around beating up skinheads because they think we are a bunch of troublemakers. Well, all I can say is let them come our way!" He beat his fist hard against his chest and spoke with a strong, authoritative tone. "We'll slaughter their little arses if we come across them. 'Cos we are fuckin' unbreakable! DO YOU HEAR ME! FUCKIN' UNBREAKABLE!"

Like sheep, the crowd followed Archie's words, "Unbreakable! Unbreakable! Unbreakable!"

Archie lifted his right leg and brought it back down to the ground with a hefty stomp. His DMs boot produced an echo around the workshop. He then stretched out his right arm to perform the Nazi salute. "Heil Hitler!"

In unison, every skinhead followed the actions of their leader, "Heil Hitler!"

Archie was satisfied with the crowd's response and his speech. He had nailed it. He had them exactly where he wanted. "So, I've many plans and ideas on how we're going to make the foreigners' lives hell. But for now...we party! What are we waiting for? Let's get that fuckin' music back on and 'ave a right old fuckin' knees up!"

The loud music filled the workshop, and within seconds, every skinhead was head-banging to a party that would go on until the early hours of the morning. Archie grabbed two tins of beer, clicked them both open with his thumbs, slanted his head back and started downing the contents, both at once, spilling the intoxicating liquid uncontrollably over his face and down his clothes.

The crowd roared and cheered on their leader, "Archie! Archie! Archie!"

After he'd drained both cans, Archie belched loudly, then he started to chant, as he barked his words out with a concoction of hatred and passion. "Time for war! Time for war!" He sang as he felt his patriotism flow through his body, "Rule, Britannia! Britannia, rule the waves!"

The crowd followed. "Britons never, never, never will be slaves...Rule, Britannia! Rule, Britannia!"

Archie was now convinced that he and his skinhead comrades were all ready for the battle to commence. The time had finally arrived.

CHAPTER 5
LITTLE INDIA: 1977

WHILE GROWING UP IN RANGAL ROAD, I always felt as if our house was like a 'Little India' surrounded by the outside Western World. We never had a dining table and would traditionally eat our meals sat cross-legged on the floor, just like my dad had done in India. We loved having meals as a family and made the most of it when Dad was at home and not working. That wasn't often because he had to work long hours to fight the increasing financial pressures of the 1970s recession. All five of us, Dad, Mum, Bob, our two-year-old sister Sharan, and I would cosy up on our living room floor together and enjoy Mum's fantastic home-cooked Indian dishes.

Mum occasionally cooked English food, but nothing too involved, merely sausages, beans, eggs - just basic stuff, as she didn't learn to cook any real English dishes until later. For our main evening meal, she would present a homemade, tasty Indian recipe. Her mother had taught her well, and she was an expert in Indian cuisine. We never had stews, chips, or roast dinners at home, so we relished them whenever we had school dinners. We always looked forward to the yearly school festive roast at Christmas, because during those years, this was the only time we would experience a traditional British meal. It was great, and we loved it!

Mum and Dad always reminded us that we had

to follow all the Indian traditions, although we were in Britain. They said it was essential for us to live with both cultures, and we should never forget that we are also Indian. We understood that. We enjoyed many of the Indian traditions, but there were some that we hated! One practice we really disliked was having to wear flip-flops inside the house. In the early years, we were not allowed to wear socks or shoes inside the house, and they had to be left out in the hallway. Mum and Dad said wearing socks and shoes around the house was too Western. So, it was either be barefoot or wear flip flops. We could manage during the British summer, but our feet would freeze like hell in the winter!

Wearing flip flops for Dad, as a youngster living near the equator, was normal, but in Britain, the weather was no comparison to the scorching heat of the Punjab. We tried to explain this to our parents, but it fell on deaf ears; they just didn't understand. We weren't allowed to wear socks to bed either! Apparently, it wasn't considered an Indian thing to do. During winter, Bob and I would sneakily roll our socks back on under the sheets as soon as our parents had gone to sleep. We had to wear socks because our little toes would turn into little blocks of ice without them.

Like most houses in Britain of the time, we didn't have central heating. The built-in living room heater smelled of gas whenever clicked on: Dad considered it dangerous. So, he purchased a two-bar electric heater, but using it cost a fortune in electricity. As a result, Dad only allowed us to keep it on for an hour before bedtime. Once the heater was off, the only thing that kept us warm were our socks and the amazing life-saving hot water bottles we were given during the depths of winter. Today, every time my baby daughter Alisha takes her hot water bottle and snuggles up with it in bed, it always reminds me of the days I did the same during my childhood.

Most people in the area had their toilets in brick sheds at the bottom of the garden. This was something else we disliked, especially when it snowed! Walking through the wet, icy snow, heading for the garden toilet wearing just flip-flops was no fun. Our feet would become blue and numb. Only after sitting near the heater inside the house for ages did we start to feel any life in them again, as they slowly returned to their original colour. Dad lived by example, and he, too, would walk through the snow wearing his flip-flops when he went to the toilet. Despite Mum's efforts to always clear the garden pathway with hot water and a spade, it would only take a short while for the cleared path to get covered in more wet snow during the heavy snow season. We'd notice Dad put on a brave face as we watched him through the window, heading toward the toilet. Even with squelchy snow in and around his bare feet and flip-flops, he didn't even flinch.

We would be shocked when we saw kids on TV wearing trainers and socks in their houses, as in our house, it was a major crime to do so! We would envy these kids and wish we could do the same. But Mum and Dad insisted we left our shoes and socks in the hallway because that's where they belonged. We hated it to begin with, but as time went on, the flip-flops became the norm. Luckily for us, as the years went on, Dad himself found it impossible not to wear socks inside the house, especially during winter. He finally relented, which meant we could, too.

Today, Bob still wears flip-flops, sandals, or even sliders, irrespective of the season or weather, except when at work. It became so ingrained and second nature for him, but not for me. Even as a grown adult, I still don't like my feet getting cold. Watching Bob wearing any of this footwear takes me back to when we lived on Rangal Road, our 'Little India'.

Another rule Mum and Dad insisted on was that we spoke Punjabi and not English within our home. This was done to ensure we learnt to say our family's native tongue. Our parents explained that we could speak English outside the house, except when visiting relatives. But at home, it was Punjabi all the way. Whenever our parents caught us speaking English, we were told off. Having said that, Bob and I spoke English to each other when neither parent was listening. In hindsight, I have to thank Mum and Dad as today their three children are fluent in Punjabi; otherwise, we would've never learnt the language without this rule.

Adherence to these rules and traditions meant we felt like we lived double lives, one in 'Little India', which was our home and another outside the house in England. To tell you the truth, being brought up with two sets of values from two cultures at the same times confused the hell out of us. But, as time went on, we learned and adapted accordingly, we had no other choice.

Understandably, after a tough day of being bullied and harassed by teachers and other kids at school, I'd feel so relieved when I got home. Being a religious family, we had many holy pictures adorning the house - ten Sikh Gurus, the Golden Temple, Sai Baba, and the Hindu gods all over our walls inside the home. Stepping into 'Little India', was like entering a Temple or Shrine of worship, where everything was safe. Peace and harmony surrounded me instantly, and there'd be no more pain; calmness descended. The cruelty of the external world was over until I next ventured outside. Our house always had a constant flow and scent of rogan josh flowing through the rooms due to Mum's cooking. It was like walking through a peaceful Bazaar in India. Unfortunately for us, this smell, which inevitably lingered on our clothes, was not met kindly at school; all the teachers and kids told us that we stank. At that time, such Indian authentic scents were unrecognised by the White-British people. We didn't care; we loved it!

Our parents taught us always to be hospitable and told us that it was customary for us as Indians to help each other and others. Bob and I would help bring out the dishes at mealtimes while Dad entertained baby Sharan. We did the same whenever we had guests; biscuits were served, and Indian tea was traditionally made. Despite Mum telling us not to touch the biscuits until the guests had helped themselves, there were always a few missing by the time the plate reached our guests. We'd discreetly eat one on route, then slip another in our trouser pocket for later.

I loved watching Mum make Indian tea; it was totally fascinating, colourful and cultural. First, she'd fill up a saucepan halfway with water, bring it to a boil and then add milk and tea leaves. Then she once again waited for it to come to the boil, but this time with the tea leaves and milk. Once this happened, she would sieve it into another saucepan. The next step was my favourite part of the process; she'd hold the empty saucepan in one hand, and in her other hand, she held the saucepan containing the brewed tea. Then she took turns and raised each pot with a theatrical flourish so the tea would travel from one saucepan to another, taking turns pouring in an extended liquid arch again and again. She'd repeat this cycle four to six times in a process known as 'pulling the tea'. I found watching her do this to be a uniquely peaceful and tranquil experience. Learnt from her mother, this technique was handed down through the generations and served the purpose of increasing the tea's flavour. While visiting India, I've come across many side-street food stalls pulling tea, and I still find it so fascinating. The art amazes me so much that sometimes I watch the masters of 'Pulling the Tea' from around the world on YouTube. They are so highly skilled in this fascinating process.

After witnessing this great Indian tradition of making tea, I found it amazing how Mum would pour the brewed tea into her English ceramic traditional teapot, and dress it up with her knitted, British-based, West Ham United Football Club tea cosy. This is just one example of exactly how the formation of East-meets-West began in our 'Little India' house, all that time ago, and would definitely branch out more through the coming years in all different areas of our lives. Up to this very day, Indian tea made in this way, for me, always tastes tantalisingly amazing.

From the day my mother first stepped foot on British Soil at the age of five, in the 1940s, she never wore any British clothes: no skirts, trousers, shirts or anything resembling Western culture. Our garden washing line always displayed one of Mum's extravagant, coloured Sari's or Salwar Kameez's - Indian clothes designed for women - flickering away in the wind. As a kid, I remember watching her multi-coloured clothes dance with the wind, making the washing line look like a man-made rainbow. It was spectacular and represented our beautiful 'Little India'. Whenever my mum went out wearing these Indian clothes during the 1970s, she was met with intrigue and fascination from non-Indian locals. Many were interested to know more about her culture and how she artistically wrapped her Sari around herself. Putting on a Sari is definitely an art form and isn't easy. But unfortunately, we were living in a very prejudiced era and location, which meant the majority of people would laugh and ridicule her for what she was wearing, just like they did with my dad's turban and our hair plaits.

When Mum was growing up, she spent many hours working on market stalls in East London with her dad, where she learnt to speak the local English cockney dialect. Based on her Indian attire, many individuals fell into the trap of thinking that she couldn't speak English, and ridiculed her with comments like, "Oi! Why you wearing weird clothes Paki lady! You're in England now! Not fuckin' Paki Land!"

Despite her diminutive stature - barely over five feet tall – my Mum's response made grown men stumble and stutter for words with fright.

"Who d'ya think you're talking to!" Her response would first shock and surprise the racists. So, she would repeat, "I SAID WHO DO YOU THINK YOU'RE BLOODY TALKING TO!"

It was great watching her in action, throwing out her totally unexpected English words at these racist individuals. During my childhood, I even saw her stand up to six-foot skinheads and hooligans when they tried to take the Mickey out of us. I don't know how she did it, but she was brave. Once these racists, caught by surprise, heard Mum talk, they'd actually get scared and scarper like cowards. Bob and I loved it and would giggle as we saw our mum bark them away.

Mum was proud of being Indian and proud of our culture and heritage just like we all were, and therefore she didn't let anyone put her down. To this day Mum still never wears any English clothes. And Sharan, my sister did much the same until the late 1980s, when Asian women began to venture out and started to wear English clothes; indicative of how both English and Indian cultures were converging. However, it took many years before Asians became an accepted, integrated part of Britain.

Despite the ridicule Bob and I faced outside our house, we knew our home was our shrine, our temple, our safe haven—our 'Little' India'. Little did we realise at the time that the peace, comfort, and safety of Rangal Road would be very short-lived.

CHAPTER 6
FROM BAD TO WORSE

THE WORKING ENVIRONMENT OF the glass factory, where Dad worked, sunk to new depths of viciousness. Both management and employees belittled immigrant workers to an extreme, even referring to them by the demeaning name 'The Jungle Mob'. They were banned from operating machinery and told that those jobs were for privileged white workers only. The ethnic workers were given grim tasks like cleaning the stubbornly stained machines and mopping the floors. Daily spot checks carried out by racially motivated managers were always negative, irrespective of the hard work and effort the immigrants put into their practice. The managers would moan and tell them they'd done a lousy job and threaten them with dismissal. The ethnic workers knew their approach to work wasn't at fault, but it was mainly due to who they were. As far as the bosses were concerned, they were foreigners who didn't belong in British society and were all treated like second-class citizens.

19th November 1977.
On this day, Dad was back from work earlier than usual. Mum was shocked to see him. "Why are you home so early? Your shift doesn't finish until six, and

it's only two o'clock in the afternoon? Is everything okay?"

Dad's pride stood him up straight, "Now they want us to clean the toilets as well. We don't mind sweeping the sticky floors, cleaning messy machines, but now they've pushed us too far! Why do Indian and black workers have to clean toilets and not white employees? They get all the best jobs, and we get all the rubbish ones. I've dignity and respect for myself. We no longer stood for it, so some of us walked out today! Including me...'

Although Dad never really talked about the daily abuse handed out at work, Mum knew it was happening; it was written all over his face when he came home. Mum wasn't surprised he'd walked out; she could only imagine the hardships he'd gone through.

But on this day, things were different. She felt that having made a stand with the racists, he'd regained his dignity. His face was no longer gloomy but bright and vibrant.

Mum had a stream of negative thoughts running through her head: How will we pay the mortgage? How are we going to survive? But not once did she let on or air her concerns. She knew and understood that Dad had faced much hardship and injustice at the factory, and his only crime was that he was an Indian and wore a turban.

Though worried, she kept calm, held his hand, and smiled warmly. "The kids will be home from school soon. Let's surprise them by making their favourite chicken curry, using your Dada (granddad)

Heera Singh's lovely secret recipe!"

Dad went into the kitchen to place his Tiffen container on the worktop. "That sounds like a great idea!"

Mum smiled courageously as she gathered fresh tomatoes, "Oh good! You can chop up the onions... Don't worry about work, I am sure something will come along. It always does."

Dad removed his turban and placed it on its regular spot on top of the telly. Then, he came back into the kitchen and grabbed two onions. "Me, Bhupinder, Adekunle, Khan and a few others - the so-called 'Jungle Mob' - bloody walked out, we did! Enough was enough!"

"Employers like that don't deserve you..." Mum shook her head erratically as she passed Dad the chopping knife.

"I can operate the machines. I saw them. They weren't difficult to use! I could have been trained as the rest could have, but they never gave us a chance." Dad took his anger out on the onion as he thoroughly chopped away.

"Hey, don't worry! I'm sure something else will come up. Waheguru (God) has put us here, and I know he'll support us and show us the way. You're not lazy; you're a hard worker, Raj. Let's get this curry made and have a great evening as a family." She knew it wasn't going to be easy for Dad to find a job due to his limited English and being a turban-wearing Indian, but she put on a brave face and continued to smile.

Dad halted his chopping; slowly, he lifted his gaze to her and let out a deep sigh before finally returning her smile.

Mum giggled as she nudged and mocked him gently, "Now come on, Mr Raj Singh! Those onions aren't going to chop themselves, are they?"

Dad and his colleagues never returned to the glass factory. This was the first time ever that my dad had stood up against racism. He didn't have a choice; none of them did. Their dignity and pride were at stake. I was so proud of my dad and the others for making that stand.

Mum was so right! Within two weeks, Dad and his friends found work at a plastics factory in East Ham. At this point, there were seven off them. As the years passed, whenever one found a better job, the others would follow suit. They moved from factory to factory, warehouse to warehouse as a group. Over time the collection grew from seven to twenty! They were all clearly an elite group of hardworking individuals and true pioneers of their time.

♦♦♦

16th August 1978.
My dad and uncle Bhupinder shared a car while they worked at the plastics factory. Today, it was Uncle Bhupinder's turn to pick up Dad. As Dad waited outside our house on Rangal Road at five in the morning, he kept an eye on the time. Bhupinder was late again! Frustrated, Dad's attention was drawn to the booming music, mixed with the noise of people shouting from across the main road. The source was the old sweet shop once owned by Mr Khan on Barking Road, but now no longer a shop. Rumours

were that the Skinheads had verbally abused and physically attacked Mr Khan so often he'd no choice but to shut up shop and return to Pakistan. It now appeared that these skinheads had taken over the shop as their latest residence, their new den, where they frequently partied into the early hours.

Reluctantly, Dad glanced over his shoulder and looked in the direction of the sound just as three skinheads came out of the shop's old front door. The music got louder, accompanied by an out-of-tune drunk trying to sing along somewhere from inside the den. Dad noticed the skinheads were all holding cans of Special Brew beer. Not wanting to draw their attention, he looked away instantly - they seemed like trouble. Rechecking his watch, he whispered angrily to himself, "Bloody Bhupinder! Always late!"

Dad felt the skinhead's glare of hatred. Archie Skipper showed his disgust toward Dad by letting loose a large deposit of phlegm at him. His Lieutenants Tommy Gatsby and Robbie Marsh shared Archie's horrid feelings.

The General began to hurl abuse towards my dad. "Oi! Paki! Why don't you just piss off back to where you fuckin' came from?"

All three men grinned and smirked as they swigged their beers. Dad tried his best to ignore them, but it was hard.

"Oi! Turban head! Didn't you fuckin' hear me?" Archie persisted.

The yelling caused Dad's heartbeat to quicken. He anxiously scanned up and down the road for Bhupinder. Although he did not need to do so, he nervously kept pushing the strap of his work rucksack up onto his shoulder.

Fortunately, within a few seconds, Dad heard the rattling sound of Bhupinder's exhaust pipe coming from his Maxi car as he approached. For the first time ever, Dad was relieved to hear the noise of Bhupinder's dilapidated, poorly maintained car.

Undaunted, the shouting from Archie and his crew got louder, "Get out of our country, you fuckin' weirdos! And take your stinkin' rotten food with yah! We don't want you or your food in our fuckin' country! You fuckin' stinkers!"

As Bhupinder pulled up, Dad literally jumped into his car, "You are always late Bhupinder!"

Bhupinder had never seen Dad get into his car so rapidly, "You know I always am Raj, my beloved wife likes to take her time with my Tiffen, you know, she fills it up with her lovely cooked food, the only problem being she takes to bloody long." Bhupinder smiled as he tried to make light of the situation, but it just didn't work at all. "Raj...are you okay? You look like you have just seen a ghost?'

"I have seen something worse than a ghost Bhupinder! Just drive, man! Them bloody skinheads across the road look like they are looking to cause trouble!"

"Yeah! That's right! Just fuck off back to the jungle you smelly Paki's!" Archie and his cronies crossed over Barking Road and began to stroll toward Bhupinder's car.

Bhupinder noticed the skinheads approaching, so he breathed in his overweight stomach which had been leaning on the steering wheel, sat up straight, slapped the car in gear and drove off as fast as he could. The rattling sound of his exhaust faded away as they gained distance. The rowdy skinheads jeered as they strolled back into their den.

As soon as Dad got to work, he used the phone box outside the factory to call Mum. He told her about the skinheads and asked her to keep an eye on them when Bob and I left for school that morning. Fortunately, by the time school arrived, the skinheads had finished partying and had all crashed out. Cautiously, Mum thoroughly checked outside our front door to make sure it was safe for us to walk to school.

Following this incident, whenever Bhupinder was driving them to work, Dad waited inside the house. He was conscious of the skinheads hanging around outside and staring menacingly in the direction of our home. As soon as Dad heard the rattling sound of Bhupinder's exhaust approaching, he'd leave the relative safety of the house. Dad found that Archie and his skinhead comrades were hanging about outside their den, whether he was working early or late shift. They seemed to know his work patterns and deliberately waited for him. The skinheads usually threw verbal abuse, and over time, this escalated to them throwing missiles like beer cans or anything else to hand. Bhupinder encouraged Dad to call the police, but he refused, hoping that if he ignored the skinheads, they'd eventually get bored and go away. That didn't happen.

♦♦♦

13th September 1978.
On this day we went to visit our Nan who lived locally on Barking Road. Bob and I loved travelling in Dad's white Hillman Hunter Estate; it was enormous inside, with really comfortable seats. Dad mainly used the car for work, so any opportunity to ride in it was a real treat. At Nan's, the grownups chatted while we played Monopoly, chess and completed a few puzzles upstairs with our uncles and cousins. Time flew by, and suddenly it was past midnight. Dad eventually said it was time for us to go home.

At around 1 am, as we neared our home in the Hillman with all five of us on board, including baby Sharan, Dad slammed on the brakes, making us lurch forward. He quickly switched off the headlights and halted the car in the middle of the road, just a few yards from our house.

Dad leaned over the steering wheel and peered towards the skinhead's den on the far side of Barking Road. Sitting in the back seats, me Bob and I couldn't see and wondered what all the fuss was about. Sharan was fast asleep in Mum's lap in the front passenger seat, and I was seated behind her. I glanced over her shoulder, and the sight made me gasp. There must have been about fifteen skinheads, all with shaven heads, wearing their braces and boots, standing outside the abandoned sweet shop, swearing and shouting. For them, this was typical behaviour, but for us, it was exceptional and disconcerting.

Mum turned to Dad and squinted, "You okay Raj? Please tell me what the heck you're doing?"

Dad slowly turned his head toward Mum; his

eyes were now wide with fear, "Skinheads! Lots of them! More than I've ever seen before hanging outside their den! They are very bad people! Dangerous!" He pointed his finger at the windscreen, his face now ashen.

Bob and I strained to see in the back seats; it was the first time we'd heard the word Skinheads, and we were curious.

"Just park up!" Mum insisted, "Let's all get inside the house. NOW!" She began to sound a bit hysterical.

Dad totally ignored her and continued to stare in front, "There are so many of them!"

As we watched the rowdy skinheads, we became aware of their loud music. It seemed to have no rhythm, it was unpredictable, and the singer was just yelling out the lyrics.

Mum was getting impatient, "Come on! Get a grip Raj! Sharan's sleeping, and we don't want to wake her up. Park the car properly and let's all get inside the house."

Dad calculated his next moves and turned on the engine, but not the headlights; he slowly moved the car forward and manoeuvred it directly outside our house. Eventually, it came to a halt.

His gaze didn't shift from the group of yobs. He whispered to Mum, "Okay, we do this quietly. You go first, Prabhjit. Take Sharan. Slowly open the front door and get inside. Then, I'll bring the boys."

Mum rolled her eyes, "Will you stop it, please! You're scaring the boys and me. You're making it sound like some sort of a military operation!"

She was so right; Dad's behaviour was scary. I

glanced at Bob; open-mouthed, he was rubbing his hands together, and it seemed he had developed a nervous twitch on the side of his face after hearing Dad's words. I felt a sudden and urgent need to go to the toilet; it was as if I was about to poo my pants. My nerves were on edge, and I could feel sweat running down my forehead. I think Bob was experiencing the same thoughts as I was; that these so-called skinheads were going to brutally attack us any moment now.

Dad attempted to calmly explain to Mum, "Let's just say that these skinheads are not nice, we need to get inside as quickly as we can. They hate Indians. Whether I'm on an early or late shift, they watch me as I go to work. Standing outside their den, as the locals call it, it seems they are planning something!"

Hearing Dad say that the skinheads were 'planning something' did absolutely nothing to appease Bob's twitch or my fears; we were now more petrified than ever. These were not words that an eight-year-old and nine-year-old should have been listening to. Me and Bob were wearing T-Shirts, and despite it being a very warm night, we both noticed the goose bumps on our arms.

"That's enough!" Mum said, taking control. She turned and faced me and Bob, "Jag! Bob! It's okay boys we are going to be just fine. Don't pay any attention to what your dad is saying."

Bob flashed me a very concerned look; we didn't share her confidence at all.

♦♦♦

Sitting on what was once a pristine white sofa, now heavily stained with beer spills, fag ash and goodness knows what, Archie Skipper swigged back the last dribble out of his Special Brew can. After tossing the empty can to the floor, he closed his eyes and started to head-bang to the heavy music that was playing in the background inside the den.

Robbie Marsh came barging in, "Archie! Guess what I just saw? That Paki family on Rangal Road 'ave just parked up. Fancy giving them a scare?"

Like the rest of his crew, Archie had been drinking, popping pills and smoking weed. His sense of restraint was long gone, while his sense of aggression surged.

He opened his eyes wide, pushed his head forward, grinned and stood up, "Why fuckin' not? Right! Let's teach these bastards a fuckin' lesson!"

Both men left the den to join the other skinheads outside on the pavement.

Despite Mum's frustration with Dad's actions in the car, she kept her cool—she always did. Mum opened the front passenger door and carried Sharan as fast as she could toward the front door. She purposely avoided looking in the direction of the skinheads. At that precise moment, Sharan woke up and instantly began to cry.

Inside the car, we all watched in horror as the events unfolded. Bob and I remained quiet as mice in the back, listening to each other's heavy, anxious breathing.

Archie was standing across the road with his lieutenants and many other skinheads by his side.

They were all staring in our direction. I looked into Archie's eyes; I could see anger and hate.

In a trembling whisper, I asked Dad, "Why's that very big man looking at us, Dad?"

Dad had already spotted Archie and his louts. He didn't respond to me because he didn't know how to.

Meanwhile, Mum struggled with a wailing baby in her arms, trying to unlock the front door.

I no longer wanted to go to the toilet; it was as if fear had taken over my whole body and frozen my insides.

Eventually, Mum made it into the house, and Dad wasted no time; he sprung out of the car, opened the back passenger door and begun to shepherd us out, "Quick boys! Both of you! Now!"

Tommy Gatsby lobbed a half-full can of Special Brew toward us. It missed Dad's head by a few inches and landed at his feet, squirting beer all over the driver's door of the Hillman.

"Bob and Jag! Inside now! You need to move faster!" Once we were out of the car, Dad slammed the vehicle's door, locked it, and grabbed our hands. All three of us charged toward our front door. That was my last straw; the desperate feeling of needing the toilet came rushing back. I couldn't hold myself any longer. I was on the verge of crapping myself.

Robbie Marsh yelled out to Dad, "Oi! Paki! Wait a minute! We wanna have a quick word with yah', wait for us!"

The other skinheads joined in, "Oi Paki! Wait for us! We only wanna chat!"

Dad had no intention of chatting; he knew exactly

what they meant by a chat.

Three of the men crossed over the main road and started to jog toward us, sniggering away. Dad saw them heading in our direction and instantly knew that this meant trouble. He grabbed Bob by the back of his T-shirt and literally threw him into the house. Then Dad turned around to find me. I was just standing at the kerb, frozen with fear, watching the three men heading in our direction. I tried to move, but despite my efforts, my muscles remained seized.

Dad shook my shoulders hard to snap me out of it. He screamed at me frantically, snapping me out of my seizure, "Come on, Jag! Inside! Now!"

The trio were closing in… fast. Dad had no choice but to lift me up and launch me at Mum, who was standing in the doorway. By now, Mum was well aware of the fact that she should never have taken Dad's cautious words that he had spoken in the car earlier so lightly. The skinheads realised that in a few steps, we'd reach safety. As an act of desperation, and without hesitation, all three skinheads tossed their beer cans in our direction.

Bob heard the commotion at the front door from where he sat on the sofa rocking Sharan in the living room, where Mum had ordered him to stay. He was trying his best to stop her wailing and to keep himself from crying at the same time.

To add to the cacophony, Mum screeched at Dad, "Quick, get in here, now! They're coming!" Then came a thudding sound, followed by another, then another, as beer can missiles crashed into the house above our front door. They could have easily landed on our heads;

instead, plumes of beer sprayed everywhere – on us, the front door, and the pavement. And it stunk, to boot.

Glancing back, aided by the glare of the streetlamp, I caught sight of the leader's Swastika tattoos on his head, just before Dad slammed the front door shut. My mind raced; I wished I were older and physically stronger so that I could've supported Dad and stood up to these hooligans. I felt so sorry for my parents, alone and defenceless as they sought to protect us from these savages.

I remember thinking, "You just wait! One day... One day I'll be strong enough to take you all on! I am gonna get the lot of yah, bloody skinheads... one day!"

From the other side of the front door, Archie roared his dreaded words, which I'll never forget: "We're gonna get you turban head! You and your fuckin' stinkin' Paki family best fuck off...or we'll burn your fuckin' house down!"

Dad double-locked the front door as we all heard a barrage of fists and kicks being delivered to it from the skinheads outside. The din coming from outside was scary; I was convinced the door would submit to the onslaught.

The insults didn't abate either, "Oi! Turban head! Open the fuckin' door! Come outside! We wanna have a fuckin' word with you!"

We all knew very well; this was not a friendly invite. Petrified, we stood motionless, but our hearts thumped away in our chests as we waited to see what they'd do next.

Our luck was in; within seconds, we heard

police sirens coming from Barking Road.

With a fearful reaction, Mum ran toward the telephone in the living room and grabbed its handset. She was about to dial 999, but Dad snatched the phone off her, "What are you doing Prabhjit?"

"What do you think I am doing? I am calling the bloody police, that's what I am doing! I am going to report what has just happened! We were attacked!"

Dad feared more trouble, "No, you mustn't! If you do that, then things will only go from bad to worse!"

Following Dad's caution, we all heard the sirens get louder, and with them, the banging on our front door ceased. With bated breath and racing hearts, we waited, unsure of what was going on outside. The silence was as unsettling as the noise. For confirmation, Dad pressed his ear to the door, listened, and shook his head; he couldn't hear the skinheads anymore, and none of us could.

We still had no idea what was going on outside. With a flash of inspiration, Dad struck out for the stairs and hurried upstairs. We all followed him like train carriages on a railway track. Bob was the last to appear upstairs, cradling a pacified Sharan in his arms.

Sneaking around our home like criminals and fearing for our lives, we managed to manoeuvre into a ringside position and peered out at the road from one of the upstairs bedroom windows. Dad told us to switch all the lights off so we couldn't be spotted. The only illumination we had came from the streetlight across the road.

As we watched, we saw two police patrol cars park directly outside the skinhead's den. We thought maybe someone locally must have seen what was going on and notified the police. Knowing that law enforcement had arrived was like a breath of fresh air.

From our vantage point, we could see the officers trying to talk to Archie and the others. The skinheads were having none of it and kept yelling and swearing and generally acting hostile. Not wanting to make things worse, the police spoke softly using non-offensive language. While the drunken skinheads kept barking at them, "Fuck off coppers! You fuckin' pigs! Fuck off!!"

Some of the skinheads scarpered as soon as the law turned up. Those who remained continued to hurl abuse at them, and the situation appeared to be turning nasty. Like cavalry to the rescue, a barrage of blaring sirens and flashing blue lights announced the arrival of three more police vehicles. Simultaneously, they descended and screeched to a halt. The reinforcements jumped out of their erratically parked cars and started to handcuff the skinheads and bundle them into the prisoner transport vehicles. However, rather than quelling the mayhem, the protests of the skinheads grew louder as half a dozen officers raided their den.

Running down the road, a swarm of skinhead reinforcements arrived to add to the disorder, and a major riot broke out. It was total chaos. Mum took Sharan downstairs into the living room and switched the telly on to drown out the commotion for her baby girl. Dad told Bob and me to go downstairs and get ready for bed, as tomorrow was a school day. Actually, it was a Saturday, but Dad wasn't thinking straight, unsurprisingly like the rest of us. Bob and I didn't budge.

The three of us stayed glued to the upstairs bedroom window until the final police car drove away and peace returned. No words were spoken; we all kept our thoughts to ourselves as we tried to make sense of what had just happened. The pressing need for the toilet forced Bob and me to race into the garden. Bob won; luckily for me, he wasn't too long. Our physical need was quickly met, but not our mental and emotional needs. The skinheads' attack, their attempts to break into our 'Little India', and our loss of safety were all very alarming for two primary school-aged children to witness firsthand.

Even though it was now dead quiet outside, we remained silent. Disheartened and worried, Dad slowly followed us downstairs to rejoin his now changed family.

That night, we saw a different side to our dad, a side we'd never seen before. Dad had always been non-violent, peaceful and easy-going. Once we were finished using the toilet, Bob and I returned to the house. With no dad insight, we ran back to the upstairs bedroom. He was already up there, but we were taken aback by what we saw. He'd changed into his pyjamas and was wearing his West Ham woolly hat with the traditional claret and blue colours that Mum had knitted for him earlier this year. He wore it every night when he went to bed. But what we found totally bizarre was that he was holding a hammer in his right hand as he stared out the window. Also, he'd fetched the wooden chair from downstairs and placed it near the window, making it the only furniture in this cold, dark and otherwise empty room. Dad stood staring out of the window, seemingly oblivious to everything else. He was motionless, and his eyes were vigilantly focused on the view outside. Seeing Dad like that reminded me of a scene from a 1970s Hammer House of Horror movie when someone was just about to hammer someone to death! It was scary!

Dad realised we were standing behind him, "Go down, you two! Get some sleep." His eyes remained focused on the street as he continually scanned the area.

Before we had time to move, Mum entered the bedroom with Sharan comfortably in her arms.

Seeing Dad, she was stern and direct: "What the hell are you doing, Raj? Come downstairs. You need to sleep! Now!" Then she spotted the hammer. Why the hell are you holding that?"

"No! Tonight, I'll stay awake... they may come back... the... skinheads may..." The words stuck in his throat.

"The police have arrested them Raj, please come."

"NO!" Dad wasn't going to budge, and from the tone of his voice, Mum knew he was adamant.

The moment deserved a camera; Dad holding his hammer, looking out of the window like a stalker, Mum cradling Sharan, Bob and I with our little worried faces. This image was a powerful representation of our childhood, to a tee!

"Go downstairs! All of you! I will be fine!" Dad insisted.

All of us, including Mum, had no choice but to

go. She knew that Dad needed time to himself.

Dad sat on the chair and placed the hammer on the floor. He vowed to stay awake, to protect his family just in case the skinheads returned. We eventually left.

Sitting alone with only the glow of a streetlamp for company, Dad mockingly scoffed and imitated his relatives from India: "Go to London! 'The City of Dreams!' You will have an amazing life! It's a great place to find work, make money, buy a house and settle down with a family."

Dad shook his head side to side very slowly as he whispered to himself. "Oh, how wrong they were. How wrong!"

I found it so hard to sleep on this night, but, when I finally did, this was the night the nightmares first began. Archie's words kept circling in my head: "We're gonna get you turban head! You and your fuckin' family best fuck off...or we'll burn your fuckin' house down!"

In my nightmare, I would be lying on my bed, surrounded by fire. Despite how hard I tried to scream, no sound would come. My face reddened with the effort. There was no escape; I lay there helplessly watching the blazing fire rage on. It never actually burnt me but danced around tormenting me. I always woke up dripping with sweat, and my clothes were soaked.

Following the events of that night, two things have marked me forever: first, hearing any police car siren, even to this day, brings back daunting memories. Second, I get shivers down my spine whenever I see Special Brew cans. Coupled with racist-beer-lobbing-Nazi-skinheads living just across from our house, I concluded our childhood sucked. Could things get any worse?

◆◆◆

In the morning, Mum went looking for Dad. She found him upstairs in the chair with his chin dropped to his chest and the hammer nearby on the floor: he was snoring for England. She prayed, "Please Waheguru (God), make these troubles go away forever. This is no way for anyone to live."

Soon after, there was a knock on the front door. Through the downstairs bedroom window, I spotted an iconic 'jam sandwich' police Rover parked right outside. Mum opened the door; I listened from my vantage point.

"Morning madam, my name is Police Constable Johnson. I am sure you know there was an incident last night across the road."

I slowly crept up beside Mum in the hallway and looked up at the tall, lanky policeman standing at our front door. Dad, half asleep, quickly went downstairs, placed his turban on his head and came rushing into the hallway. Bob followed behind him. Sharan was still fast asleep.

"We received numerous anonymous phone calls last night about the skinheads across the road. They were making a lot of noise. When we turned up and told them to quieten down...they got a bit rowdy, and we had to arrest quite a few of them."

Dad softly nudged me out of the way and took my spot next to Mum. "Morning, Mr Constable; why are you telling us this?" he said defensively.

PC Johnson continued, "We also received a few phone calls to say that an Indian family on Rangal Road was being attacked. You are the only Indian family on this road, that's why I've come to see if you are all okay." Looking directly at my dad, the policeman asked, "Did the skinheads try to attack you last night and break your door down?"

I rejoiced internally. Help at last! Mum and Dad were going to tell the police about the skinheads, and they were all going to prison for a long, long time! Sorted!

Dad laughed hysterically, "What noise? Skinheads? We heard nothing. I don't know what you're talking about... Mr Constable."

The voice inside me screamed. What? Have you gone mad? Tell him, Dad, tell him everything.

The policeman took out his notepad and pen. "The thing is, sir, in order to take action against these hooligans, we need a statement from you. Otherwise..."

"We will do no such thing! Thank you, Mr Constable. We are fine..." Dad stuck to his guns.

Mum was staring daggers at Dad, and just like Bob and me, she was wondering what the hell he was doing. Many thoughts raced through my mind: Dad, why don't you just tell the PC the truth? We could have all been killed last night.

Johnson gave it his last shot, "You're the only Indian family on this road...and the reports said..."

"No, Mr Constable! We are fine," Dad repeated

assertively.

PC Johnson firmly placed his notepad and pen back into a shirt pocket. "Okay, but can I please give you some advice..."

Like us, Mum was flabbergasted and still trying to digest Dad's untruthful words. She gave Dad a penetrating stare before acknowledging the constable, "Yes, please..."

"You see that derelict shop across the main road." The PC pointed toward Barking Road, "A nasty lot of skinheads live there, it's their den. They are involved in all types of drugs... They hate people who..." He stopped himself, "Let's say they're not friendly at all. This isn't a safe place for you and your family to live."

Great! Just what Bob and I needed to hear!

The PC shifted his weight from foot to foot. "...If it's possible, I advise you to move away to a safer location."

After hearing these words, Dad lost it! His anger got the best of him. "Are you asking me to leave my house? I've worked day and night to get this property! I came to this country with nothing! I have the right to build my dream! You dare tell me to leave!"

Dad slammed the door shut abruptly. "We are fine. Thank you, officer." his voice trailed away.

After the police visit, Mum and Dad argued all day. Mum wasn't happy that Dad hadn't told the truth, while Dad explained that if he had reported the skinheads, the trouble would only get worse. They disagreed absolutely. Mum had faith in the police, so did Bob and me. Don't get me wrong; we totally understood where Dad was coming from by not filing a complaint and wanting to keep the peace.

After this day, Dad told Mum never to step outside the house alone, but only with him present, because the streets weren't safe at all for Indians to walk freely. Bob and I wanted to move house and get away from all the skinhead bullshit. But we couldn't get ourselves to ask Dad. We knew he was still holding on to his dream of us living happily ever after on Rangal Road.

Bob and I prayed that the arrested skinheads would be sent to prison and never ever come back. But, deep down, we knew this just wasn't going to happen; they would most definitely return.

CHAPTER 7
INTIMIDATION

TWO DAYS AFTER THE TRAUMATIC skinheads incident, Dad noticed that the same skinheads had returned across the road, and were once again hanging out at their den. From then on, every day without fail, before Bob and I began our journey to school, we'd stick our heads out of the front door and thoroughly scan the area for lurking skinheads. Mum and Dad did the same. If we were going out as a family, Dad would be the first outside to check it was safe for us all to leave. This wasn't right! We were all still shocked and living in fear, dreading a potential recurrence.

At times, I'd wish I were my three-year-old baby sister, who was totally oblivious to what was happening around her. But the more I thought about it, I was actually relieved and glad that she lived in her baby world because at least she wouldn't remember the abuse we encountered. I hoped that by the time she grew up, things would've changed, and Asians would be more accepted. I could only hope.

The skinheads now knew that we were weak, undefended and yet, hadn't reported them to the police. They continued their devilment to make our lives a total living hell by planning a full-on attack. First, it all began with the leaflets. They would be anonymously posted through our letterbox. Being a kid, I loved cartoons and comic strips, but these were different. These flyers contained offensive cartoon drawings. Some had a picture of an Indian man balancing a rather over-exaggerated-sized turban on his head. Others included images of black men with large, swollen black lips and Chinese people wearing Asian rice hats with overemphasised squinted eyes. These leaflets were the ultimate form of intimidation, and they all delivered the same message written in bold: 'Get out of our country!'

The senders didn't shy away from telling us who they were; the leaflets clearly stated at the top who was responsible for these hideous written messages: The National Front. They also included their slogan, which I had seen spray-painted on many Canning Town walls as graffiti: Keep Britain White! N F Rules!

Over time, the wording on the leaflets became more offensive. They were trying to increase the level of fear and frighten us into moving out of the area. I was only eight years of age when I first saw these leaflets. Even today, I'm still shocked by what I saw back then. We already knew the word Paki as an abusive slang term for Asian-Indians as we were consistently called Paki's at school and on the streets. But, after reading these flyers, I learnt other offensive, nasty and racist words like Nigger and Chinky. The message on the leaflets was always clear and concise: 'No Niggers, Paki's or Chinkies are allowed to live in Britain. So, fuck off back to your countries, or we will kill you!' or 'If you don't leave Britain, we will burn your house down!' and 'If you don't leave our country, we are going to rape your daughters and kill your family!'

I didn't even know what the word *rape* meant at the time, but I remember thinking it must have been a bad word as it came from the skinheads. These leaflets were extremely scary to read. Every time Mum or Dad caught us with one, they'd snatch it out of our hands and would say, "Don't read these pathetic leaflets! Throw them away!"

Our parents would immediately dispose of the leaflets whenever they found them. Many years later, Mum told me that she and Dad did everything they could to ensure that we didn't read them. But since they came through the letterbox with monotonous regularity, it was impossible for Bob and me not to stumble across them. Reading these messages made us feel insecure, as if we were somewhere we shouldn't be and didn't belong in Canning Town.

♦♦♦

20th November 1978.
I will never forget the first time it happened. It must have been about 6 pm. We had finished our supper and were all relaxed in front of the telly watching the comedian Michael Crawford, playing Frank Spencer, the ever-so accident-prone character in the hit comedy series 'Some Mothers Do 'Have 'em'.' We'd regularly gather around the TV and laugh hysterically at his hilarious antics. Given the bullying at school that we were experiencing and the fear of dreaded skinheads at home, we had little to be happy about. It felt good to laugh, even if it was only for a short while. It was a kind of escapism from the reality that surrounded us.

On this particular evening, Sharan was sitting in

her baby bouncer chair, giggling away at the telly. Each time she laughed, she released a small squeaky fart. We weren't only laughing at Frank Spencer; we were also laughing at her; it was so funny...

Our enjoyment came to an abrupt end with an enormous crashing sound coming from somewhere close by. Dad jumped up from the sofa, and his laughter had evaporated. "What the bloody hell was that?" Like a man possessed, he ran to the downstairs bedroom, as the shattering noise seemed to have come from inside that room. This room had a large front window that looked out onto the road.

Surprised and confused, we all looked at each other; no one had an answer for him. Sharan's giggles had now turned into hysterical crying.

"Stay back," Dad shouted as he slowly pushed the door open.

Bob whispered, "Are we under attack by the skinheads, Dad? Are we going to die?"

"Quiet, boy!" Dad peered around the door and couldn't believe what he saw inside the bedroom, "Oh, my God!"

Me, Bob, and Mum, with Sharan in her arms, followed Dad into the room to see broken glass strewn everywhere. Despite Mum's efforts to calm her, Sharan kept shrieking, as if she sensed something was wrong.

The entire window had been shattered; glass shards littered the bed, while others were embedded in the walls from the force of impact. A large amount of glass lay on the floor, among which was the weapon used to smash it — a house brick. Mum instructed Bob and me to step back and stay in the doorway. Mum handed Sharan to Bob. Dad's flip-flops offered no protection against the jagged glass on the floor; he hurried back into the hallway to put on his steel-toe-capped work shoes. With his feet better protected, Dad returned and began to pick his way across the room, crunching as he went. Picking up the brick, he slowly turned and glanced at us; the helpless expression on his face conveyed everything. Somebody had just thrown a brick through our front window. Really? Was this actually happening? It started to seem as though Bob had been right to question whether we were under attack!

Peering out the broken window, we noticed a man standing across the street. He was wearing a white vest, long red shiny leather Dr. Martens laced boots, tight bleached jeans with red braces and had a shaven head. He calmly leant against the wall, with his hands in his jeans pockets and one leg hooked up supported by the wall behind him. The Swastika tattoos on his temples were clearly visible.

Archie held an offensive smirk and remained totally relaxed. He had made his statement, loud and clear. He showed no remorse whatsoever, and if anything, he seemed proud of his actions. Bob and I were now shivering, partly from the cold November evening air slicing through the broken window, but even more so because of our ever-growing fears.

In full rage, Dad yelled out at the skinhead, "Oi! Did you do this to my house? Did you just smash my window with this bloody brick?" He angrily waved the brick over his head

Archie Skipper stopped leaning on the wall and set off toward our house, his gaze focused directly on Dad.

He responded to Dad with sheer mockery, imitating an Indian accent while wobbling his head. "Oh, bloody, bloody!"

Then, the biggest Neo-Nazi in Canning Town replied adamantly with a smug-filled face. "Yes! Yes, I did, and guess what?" He got louder, "If you and your family don't get out of our country, we're going to fuckin' make your life hell! We're the National Front, fuckin' Neo-Nazis! We're the future! Just get out of our country and take your fuckin' stinky food with you!"

Dad was always very polite and patient, but this encounter really pressed his buttons. He spun away from the window and ran across the room, accompanied by the irritating scrunching noise of the glass on the floor. He pushed past us, like a raging animal in fury. Dad headed toward the front door, muttering to himself, "You what? You smash my window? Then you wait outside to joke at me? Wait, I'll show you! You skinhead bastard!"

My dad was of average build, and this skinhead had muscles protruding from everywhere. We all knew that in a fight, Dad wouldn't have a chance against the General, but this didn't bother him. Protecting his family required him to be brave; he just wanted to give Archie a good pounding. He was livid.

"Where are you going Raj?" Mum tried to hold Dad back, but her attempt was useless. His rage was at boiling point; he didn't even stop to put his turban on and stormed out with his hair bobble showing at the top of his head. This was not the man I thought I knew; I'd never, ever seen him leave the house before without his turban.

By the time Dad opened the front door, Archie was gone. Dad peered right, then left, but without success; Archie was nowhere to be seen.

"Where are you? Come here, you coward! How dare you attack an innocent family with young children! How dare you!" Stood in the middle of the road, Dad even started to speak and swear in Punjabi as he waved his clenched fists in mid-air. He was beside himself. "Aaja Kote!" (Come on, you dog!)

I found it weird watching Dad act like a nutter, but I totally understood how he felt. He reminded me of my favourite superhero, The Incredible Hulk. He was ready to smash Archie if he'd stuck around, but the coward was nowhere to be seen.

By now, for us, being abused by the skinheads had become the norm. But today Archie had taken their behaviour to a totally different level. He had found a new method of making our lives hell: window-smashing!

Dad eventually finished ranting and raving and came back into the house mumbling to himself, "Bloody bastard! How dare he smash our window?"

Sharan had stopped crying and was sucking on her dummy while she sat in her baby-bouncer in the living room. Mum went into the garden shed and fetched a dustpan and brush to start clearing up the mess. Bob and I were sent into the living room to take care of Sharan as our parents began to clean up the carnage in the bedroom.

Glass shards are insidious, and it took Mum and Dad ages to remove them from the bedroom walls and carpet. All we could hear was the cringing noise of glass being swept up, and Dad occasionally coming out of the room to empty the dustpan in the rubbish drums, which we kept in the garden. To drown out the sounds, Bob turned up the TV's volume. Sharan's attention was captivated by *Bagpuss*, her favourite cat character from children's TV. In the background, Bob and I could still hear the crunching of glass. We were gazing at the TV screen, but we weren't really watching it. Our minds were elsewhere, considering the consequences of what might have been. Any of us could have been in the bedroom at the time. If that brick had hit Bob or me, it could've been disastrous! Or Sharan! It didn't bear thinking about, evil bastards.

Bob and I didn't utter a single word to each other; we didn't know what to say. We were both dumb struck by the unnerving event that had taken place. I do remember thinking to myself: was this a warning from the skinheads, and if we didn't listen to their demands, were things going to get worse?

A few weeks earlier, luckily, Dad had brought home some heavy-duty green plastic sheets that his workplace was disposing of. At the time, he had thought that somehow these sheets would have been useful when he decorated the bedrooms upstairs. Now they were to serve another purpose. Dad nailed the plastic sheets from inside the house, covering the window as a temporary fix until he organised proper repairs. The sheets were very thick and robust, and you couldn't see through them, which didn't matter as none of us really wanted to see the dangers lurking outside the front of our house. It took Dad ages to nail them into place. Bob and I hated these plastic sheets; they always flapped to the dictates of the wind. This just wasn't normal.

♦♦♦

The next day, Dad organised for a fitter to replace the whole window. Within two days, another brick was thrown and smashed the glass again. Undeterred, Dad had that window replaced as well. The skinheads then resorted to an arsenal of missiles like bottles and beer cans, or anything they could get their hands on! The cycle of destruction repeated. Every time Dad replaced a window, within two or three days, it would be shattered again.

Mum had had enough. "Raj, how many more windows are you going to replace? Go to the police and report this, now!"

Dad remained adamant despite replacing thirteen windows, "No, Prabhjit, we'll not tell the police. It'll only make matters worse!"

"It's frightening our children! And me! I am sick and tired of clearing the mess up Raj. Bloody broken glass everywhere. You need to go to the police. Otherwise..." She hesitated, "I know you've worked hard for this house, but it looks like we will be left with no other choice except to move," Mum pleaded for the safety of the family.

Dad wasn't having any of it, "No! They're mere hooligans who'll eventually give up and get bored.

But..." His eyes lit up, "I do have a solution, an idea of how I can make sure they'll never ever break our window again. I have been thinking about it for days."

It turned out Dad's great idea was to cover the whole window with a wooden board. He visited the local DIY store and purchased a sheet of timber and spent the rest of the day fixing it in place. His constant hammering reverberated throughout the house. I hated this morbid board; it made the room so dark and grim. It was horrible. But for Dad, it was both a victory against the skinheads and a message to them staying he was in charge. What he didn't know was that this victory would be so short-lived.

The following morning, I remember being woken by Dad's voice coming from outside our front door. I could feel a November breeze snaking its way along the hallway and entering the living room. Bob was still snoring away on the other living room sofa. Something wasn't right. I leapt off my sofa-bed and peeped into the hallway. I noticed that the front door was wide open and wondered who Dad was talking to. I couldn't see him, but only hear him mumbling. From the kitchen, I heard Mum rattling some dishes about, so I sprinted to see her, "Mum? Where's Dad? Who's he talking to?" I was quite agitated.

Mum sighed deeply, "Go outside, and you'll..." She threw her hands up into the air, waving them erratically, "I don't know why he won't listen to me and go to the police! He keeps saying it'll stop, but it won't! It's getting bloody worse!"

I felt a nervous knot form in my stomach. "Mum, what have the skinheads done now?"

Mum looked at me and saw the anguish on my face. She remembered she was talking to an eight-year-old and toned down her reply. "Don't worry son, it's gonna be okay. Dad will be fine. He just needs some time alone."

Despite her effort to pacify me, I sensed that something was wrong.

As Mum wasn't giving me a straight answer, I reluctantly headed toward the front door. My knotted stomach tightened; I was dreading seeing what I might find. I purposely took small steps as I was in no hurry to reach my journey's destination.

As I got closer, Dad's words got clearer, "Why are they doing this to us? Why can't they just leave us alone? What are you going to do now, Raj? You cannot win! The skinheads will always win!"

I hesitantly stepped out of the house. Dad kept chatting to the board and didn't even acknowledge my presence. While talking to the boarded-up window, he was making various hand gestures and facial expressions! At that moment, I realised that I had every reason to be concerned about my broken Dad.

"How can this stop? Why don't they leave us alone?" He continued to ask the ever-listening board all these weighty questions as if he were having some sort of therapy!

Dad carried on talking to the wooden board, not even glancing in my direction. I turned to face the board and couldn't believe what I was seeing! Oh, my God! Now I understood precisely why Dad had lost the plot. The board was covered in racist graffiti: 'Paki's out!' 'NF Rules!' 'Stinky bastards!' and an extensive display of swastikas adorned the board in various colours and sizes. My poor old Dad's face was contorted with pain, disbelief, and malaise - this was the last straw. It was as if he had reached a dead end.

"Why are they doing this to us? Why?"

Due to the drama of the situation, I'd completely forgotten to wear my flip-flops. My feet were freezing from standing on the cold pavement, but I was stuck, transfixed, as I reread the racist remarks over and over again.

I wanted to run back into the house, to my sofa-bed, to pretend this wasn't actually happening and that it was just another nightmare. But I couldn't; I knew that I had to do something to help Dad. "Dad! Dad!" I tried my best to snap him out of it.

He eventually heard my voice and swung his head toward me. He was searching for answers. "What am I supposed to do, son? When I put up a window, they smash it! When I put up a board, they cover it with racist words. I just can't win, can I? They will always win."

I did have an answer, but it wouldn't have made a blind bit of difference to the situation, so I kept it to myself. Through the naivety of age, my answer was that I wished I were older, stronger, and an experienced fighter. Then I could've hunted those bastards down and smashed their faces in. The rage inside burned like an out-of-control fireball, but I was too young, too small and wouldn't have a chance against them. However, I did know one thing for sure: I wouldn't be young and small forever. One day, I would hunt them down one by one... all of them!

With fallen shoulders, Dad dropped his head to his chest and dragged his feet back into the house. I remember hoping I'd broken my dad's train of thought and saved him from insanity. He was crushed and defeated. Finding the graffiti plastered all over the board was totally soul-destroying for him. He felt that he had lost, and the skinheads had won. He didn't know what the hell to do next; he was at rock bottom. I felt so sorry for him, but I couldn't say anything as I didn't know what to say. I just kept looking at the Swastikas and continued to scan the abusive, horrible words until Mum eventually called me in.

The graffiti increased day by day. Within three days, the whole board was obliterated by intensely offensive racist remarks. The board became an eyesore both inside and outside the house. We hated it. Dad finally had the board taken down and once again replaced the panels with glass. His solution to the problem had failed utterly. Two weeks later, the front window was smashed again…

It's sad to say, but it actually became a routine: window gets smashed, place Sharan in the baby bouncer with a dummy, and switch the telly on for her as a distraction. Bob and I got the plastic sheets out of the garden shed, Dad and Mum would clear all the glass then hang up the plastic sheets until the window fitters were called the next day. And so it repeated. Although we got immune to this regular occurrence, it didn't mean that we weren't frightened each time it happened. In fact, the sound of shattering glass understandably scared the crap out of all of us every time it happened. When I asked my cousins, who lived in various locations, if they got their windows vandalised, they were shocked. Their answer was no. Likewise, when we asked the same question to the other white kids in school, again, the answer was no. It was only happening to us.

On the other hand, some of the racist kids in school turned around and said, "Well, of course, your windows are gonna get smashed, you deserve it. After all, you're Paki's!"

There seemed to be an unseen dark cloud over our house. Mum and Dad were now always arguing because Dad would not go to the police or move house. Me and Bob were living in shock and dreaded the next glass-invasion. We knew our 'Little India' wasn't safe anymore. But no matter what, Dad decided to stick to his guns. He wasn't going to move or go to the police. We had no choice except to endure the attacks. Every day, we all hoped and prayed that the skinheads would eventually get bored and stop hassling us.

Due to the skinheads' unpredictable and violent behaviour, our parents never allowed Bob, nor me, to go out and play with our friends after school. In fact, we weren't even allowed to play outside our very own front door! What a childhood!

Dad explained why we couldn't play outside our house, and in doing so, unintentionally terrorised the hell out of us even more, "Jag and Bob listen! It is not safe for Asians to be out on the roads. We must stay safe in our homes and keep away from these skinheads. They're bloody dangerous!"

Whenever we went out in Dad's car, I'd notice

many White-British children playing on their bikes and having fun with their friends. Unfortunately for us, this was not possible. Instead, Bob and I spent all the time while we lived at Rangal Road playing in our garden.

♦♦♦

The racism that my family and I faced in the 1970s can only be described as brutal, violent and severe. The experiences we encountered left us all with both physical and mental scars to make sure we'd never forget. Unfortunately for us, as I said before, we were in the wrong place at the wrong time. For us, the 1970s in East London were a very dark era. We were unwanted, unwelcome and ridiculed because we were different, a minority, and living in an area where the majority of the White-British people had nothing for us but hatred.

The regular abusive remarks shouted from outside our front door from racist individuals passing by became the norm. Bob and I always wondered if there was anyone out there in the world who could help us. Was there a saviour out there? Was anyone, someone, somehow going to come to our rescue? All the comic books I read at that time showed that 'Good' always prevails over 'Evil', and there was always a hero somewhere. Where was our hero? We had no choice except to live, hoping that he or she would find and save us one day.

My dad never told his family in India about the struggles we encountered. He didn't want to cause them any concern. Besides, he knew his mother,

Gurcharan, in Amritsar, would not be able to bear the bad news, as it would break her heart. From the letters he had received from his dad, Papa Kishan, my dad knew his mother's health was poor, and that telling her about the situation in England would only make matters worse. So, whenever Dad wrote to his family, he would always tell them a white lie and say everything was fine in the UK.

As this was far from the truth, Dad revealed to me many years later that he used to cry every time he wrote to his family. He felt so bad for telling them lies, but he knew it was for their own good. He just couldn't get himself to tell them the truth, that he and his family were actually living in a relentless, re-occurring nightmare...

TO BE CONTINUED...

THE 'UNBREAKABLE' SAGA CONTINUES...

TURN THE PAGE FOR AN EXCLUSIVE EXCERPT FROM BOOK TWO ...

CHAPTER 1
THE HOLOCAUST

25th November 1978.

DAD DEEPLY MISSED HIS FAMILY HE HAD LEFT behind in India. Feeling nostalgic, he decided to take out the family photos stored inside the two suitcases he brought with him when he left India for England. As he dragged out the suitcases from under his and mum's bed, I couldn't believe what I saw — Swastikas painted on either side of each case in pink nail-polish! Instantly I went into shock. The symbols were clearly visible, about ten inches long, and to me represented the skinheads, Hitler and our archenemies, the UK far-right fascist political party: The National Front.

I had grown up with this sign and I knew very well it meant trouble. I couldn't comprehend why my father had swastika symbols drawn on his suitcases. It wasn't even done discreetly; it was right in your face! My eight-year-old brain was baffled and ran off in all sorts of directions trying to make sense of what I was witnessing. Was my father an undercover Indian-Nazi spy? Was there even such a thing?

During those years we had the nasty racist teachers, bullies, and the skinheads to contend with. They made our lives a living hell, and now, to see my father openly displaying the dreaded racist symbol on his suitcases was a right eye-opener for me. Was he a traitor in disguise?

I plucked up my courage to ask him the

question, "Dad, why do you have the skinhead swastika signs on all your suitcases? Are you a member of the National Front?"

Mum, Dad and Bob silently glanced at each other before bursting out with laughter. Baby Sharan, who was frolicking on my parents' bed, noticed the three of them giggling away. She decided to join in too, even though she didn't have the slightest clue what was going on. I didn't either. It seemed as if they were mocking my question.

Here I was, flabbergasted after having seen the horrific Skinhead Nazi-German sign in my house on my very own dad's suitcases, and all they could do was laugh?! Were they all in it together? Was I the last one to know that my very own father was an Indian-Nazi spy?

After they had all finished their guffaws, Dad kindly explained. He told me that long before Hitler started to use the sign to represent the Third Reich, many other cultures, including Hinduism, had used the symbol for almost 6000 years. Dad explained that this original symbol has always represented good luck, well-being and spirituality. He said that the Nazi swastika tilted at a 45-degree angle, giving a slant to the symbol. Its arms pointed clockwise, and usually it was black on a white circle with a red background. Whereas the swastika of Hinduism and many other peaceful cultures appeared flat and balanced, often with dots or decorative elements. Dad said that the Nazi symbol is merely a manipulation of the original swastika and stands as a representation of Hitler, his Nazi party and all the wrongdoings they stood for.

Dad told me that the reason why his mother had drawn the symbols on his suitcases was so that they would provide him with all the good luck and blessings he needed on his voyage from India to England. She also said that it would be easier for Dad to recognise his suitcases when they came through the luggage carousel at Heathrow Airport. All he had to do was look for the pink Swastikas.

After taking a closer look, I soon realised that the swastika symbols on my dad's suitcases weren't at a slant, but were flat, and contained four dots within them. Phew! Thank God! I was so glad that Dad had cleared up my confusion. I was now confident that my father was not an undercover Indian-Nazi spy. What a relief!

However, I did wonder what the reaction would have been of the people at Heathrow Airport when they saw my father's suitcases come through the luggage carousel. I mean, they must have thought why the hell did this Indian man have pink swastika symbols nail-polished on either side of his suitcases. Without looking closely at the symbol, just like I hadn't, they too must have been very confused. I would have loved to have seen their faces.

♦ ♦ ♦

Mum and Dad always tried their best to give us a good education, even though we lived in a hostile environment. It wasn't easy for Bob and me to focus on our studies when we faced so much trouble around us.

My mum hardly ever went to school when she

was young. She stayed home most of the time and helped Nan raise her younger sister and three brothers. Mum was the eldest out of her siblings; therefore, she had to look after the little ones. She changed their nappies, fed them, and did all the housework. Mum didn't really enjoy going to school anyway, hence she never obtained a proper education. Back then in the UK, no one cared if you went to school or not. Thankfully, that has now changed, and the authorities are much more stringent today.

My dad also had a poor education. He wasn't the least bit interested in studying when he went to school and college in India. When both my parents reached adulthood, they regretted deeply to not have paid attention to their education when they were younger. They didn't want us to be in the same situation as when we grew up.

Although our parents didn't have the knowledge or skills to help us with our homework, they did something else for us: they gave us books to read. They didn't want us to end up like them, struggling with reading and writing for the rest of our lives. They wanted us to be better than them, smarter, and educated.

Whenever our parents went shopping, they would always buy books for us to read. For many years, it was the norm. During this time, Mum and Dad spent a lot of money on books. Eventually, their budget got tighter. Our quick-thinking mum came up with an excellent idea that we should join the local library in Canning Town, on Barking Road, to access free books. Great idea!

Bob would read all his six chosen books within days, then he'd start to hassle me for my books. I wouldn't part with them until I'd read all my six books at least three times. The only problem being that I was a terribly slow reader. Bob and I hardly ever argued or fought at home; I mean, we got enough of that crap outside our house. The only exception to this rule was my snail-paced reading skills, which frustrated Bob to no end.

"Hurry up Jag! You bloody slowcoach! You take ages reading your books!"

This was the only time he really lost it with me. If Bob had let me read rather than harangue me, I am sure I would've finished the books sooner.

Once we'd read all our library books several times, boredom kicked in. We needed more to quench our ferocious reading appetite and would beg Mum to take us to the library…again.

Mum would remember the strong advice Dad had given to her.

"No, Prabhjit, you can't take the kids to the library on your own! Those skinheads are always lurking around the streets. It's too dangerous. I will take you all in the car on my next day off work. The streets are not safe for us."

Mum didn't listen, not because she disrespected Dad but because she knew how important it was for us to gain an education. Dad was always working erratic hours to get as much overtime in as possible. He worked night and day shifts. This meant that we didn't know when he was going to be home next. Even when he was home, he was understandably too tired and just wanted to chill out or sleep most of the time.

So, Mum, being Mum, wasn't going to wait for Dad and took us to the library anyway. She wasn't scared of the skinheads.

Off we would go. Sharan would be strapped up in her pram. Me and Bob would trot along besides Mum, as we all headed to the library. Mum always made us promise not to whisper a word to Dad, because it would have upset him. We never did.

Bob and I loved the library and would get so excited about the stories we were going to get to read, and looked forward to selecting our entitlement of books. We chose very carefully. Both of us enjoyed reading so much that as soon as we got home, we would get stuck into our books straightaway. I suppose looking back, I realise now that reading was a form of temporary escapism for me and Bob, kind of like a mini-break from the horrid reality we were living.

We were always fascinated by the never-ending fantasy worlds of dragons, princes, princesses, quests, and goblins. More importantly, it was the *saviours* who caught our attention. These heroes would always come along to save the day in the stories. We too wished that we had a saviour: someone who would come and save our day. A shining knight in armour who would protect us; a shield that would be stronger than the skinheads and be on the side of righteousness.

On our way to the library, Mum always remind us, "Now listen to me, kids. If we come across any skinheads, don't look in their direction. You hear me?"

We just couldn't help ourselves and took a

discreet glance whenever we saw one. For us, they were too scary, hideous, and grotesque to be ignored.

I remember when the skinheads first moved into their new den across our road. One day as we walked past their residence, despite mum's warning to the contrary, me Bob and I discreetly had a quick peep through their curtainless windows. This was the first time we'd seen the interior of their den. We spotted numerous swastika and Hitler posters plastered all over the walls like wallpaper. It really frightened me. At that precise moment, in my eight-year-old brain, I concluded that we actually had Hitler's Nazi-German soldiers living near us. No longer were they after the Jews, now they had a new target...us — Indians. For us, it was all over! I kept these thoughts to myself for months.

Every time I saw a war-themed film, drama, or documentary on the telly, my palms would get sweaty, and I'd feel fear swimming all over my body. I now knew that one day we too would have to face a concentration camp and eventually be gassed just like the Jews. Our time on Earth was limited.

Also, whenever I watched any programme related to some sort of war, at bedtime my nightmares would intensify. I had many recurring nightmares during those years.

In one repeating, dreaded nightmare, there would be a full battalion of German soldiers wearing their feldgrau, greyish green, infantry uniform standing outside our house on Rangal Road. The loud-mouthed racist bystanders were rhythmically waving their banners into the air. Some were promoting the

German swastika emblem, and others displayed pictures of their leader and icon, Hitler.

In the nightmare, me and my family would all get dragged out of our house, one by one, whilst we cried and pleaded for mercy. Despite how much my dad begged the German officers to let his family go free, his pleas for mercy fell on deaf ears.

A grinning German general who had swastika tattoos on his temples would be standing in the road with his arms folded. It was the same skinhead who was always causing us trouble from the den across the road from our house. In my nightmare, he was wearing the German army uniform and not his customary white T-shirt, jeans, braces, and Dr. Martens boots. For some reason, the sleeves on his German army jacket were missing, exposing his bulging biceps. Maybe this image in my nightmare illustrated the mighty, dominant power of the Nazi skinheads who stood against our poor, defenceless family.

I would always be the first one to be blindfolded by the German firing squad as I bawled my eyes out. Then they would lean me up against the wall outside our house and shoot me down with their MG 42's. Without any hesitation. I would helplessly drop to the ground dead. Then, it would be Bob's turn to get shot, followed by Mum and Dad.

The horrendous nightmare would reach its climax as the Germans would aim for the last remaining survivor...my baby sister Sharan! She had watched the horrific events take place whilst strapped in her pram, her face was red with all the screaming she was doing. The merciless, sleeveless general would grin and slowly place his revolver on Sharan's head. It would always be the same. As soon as he grinned and went to pull the trigger on my wailing sister, I would literally wake up, open my eyes wide and thankfully snap out of the nightmare. Thank God!

I would immediately jump off my sofa and start to shake my head like crazy, trying to get the nightmare out of my head, whilst drenched in sweat all over. Bob's sleep was always disturbed by my behaviour as he slept on his sofa opposite me in the living room.

To tell you the truth, I lost count of the number of times I had this recurring frightful nightmare. Without fail, my nightmare always ended the moment it was Sharan's turn to take the bullet. After that, I would struggle to get back to sleep, afraid the nightmare might return. I would toss and turn for the rest of the night.

On the rare days when Dad was home in the evening and not doing a late shift or overtime, we would all get snuggled up in our front room on the sofas and watch the telly together. My thoughts would sometimes slip away, mainly to my Nazi-nightmare and the forthcoming holocaust. I would secretly scan all my beloved family members one by one, while their eyes were glued to the telly. Instantly, I could feel tears strolling down my cheek. I would think about the fact that once the Neo-Nazi skinheads had dragged us all out into the road and shot us one by one, we would all no longer exist. Unnoticed, I would wipe my tears as they flowed down my cheeks.

I didn't want my family to share my sadness, so I kept these thoughts to myself. I was going to miss them all. I would cry many tears, silently. I knew that if we were not killed straight away, me, and Bob would most probably be placed in some tiny rat-infested prison cell, or concentration camp after being captured by the Nazis. Dad most probably would be dead, shot, trying to protect his family and only God knows what would happen to Mum and my baby sister. The Holocaust was due! It was approaching and there was nothing we could do to stop the relentless Nazi skinheads.

Having such thoughts weren't good for an eight-year-old. Consequently, I faced many repercussions, including an eating disorder. I hardly ever felt hungry, so Mum would force me to eat, and when I did, a few hours later it would all end up at the bottom of the toilet as puke. Luckily, our boghouse was in the back of the garden, and no one ever heard me do the bulimic purging. I was glad they didn't, otherwise they would only have asked questions, and I would have ended up at the doctor's surgery.

It would take many years before I actually realised the many different ways that the skinheads, bullies and racist individuals took a negative toll on my mind, body and confidence levels during my childhood.

We would get so bored at home on the weekends when Dad was at work. That's why, despite Dad's warnings, Mum still took us out of the house when he was absent. Not only did we go to the library, but we would also visit my Nan and go shopping.

Occasionally, after visiting the library, we would pop across the road and have a wander around Rathbone Street Market. We never went too far; all the places we visited were only a short walk from our house.

We could only play in the garden for a certain time before we got bored and wanted to do something else. Mum didn't believe in being caged in by the fear of these skinheads and racists. The skinheads did not scare Mum at all and she wasn't about to be cooped up or trapped inside her own house like an animal in a cage. None of us ever told Dad about our local trips, and Mum always ensured that we got home before he finished work.

♦ ♦ ♦

30th November 1978.
Mum decided to pick us up after school. Then the four of us, Bob, Mum, Sharan, and I, strolled over to visit my Nan. Sharan was in her pram, swinging her baby legs back and forth while intriguingly scanning the scenery with her little head bopping about. Bob and I always struggled to keep up with Mum's pace. She was a very fast walker. We were not sure if it was because she wanted us to get to safety as soon as possible or if she just wanted to get to our destination and back home before Dad came back from work. We never asked. Bob and I always struggled and lightly jogged alongside her, trying our best to keep pace.

On our way to Nan's house, I spotted a small,

cozy-looking newspaper booth outside the Abbey Arms Pub. Inside the booth stood a very tall, frail, old English man, dressed in a white attire, sporting a grey flat cap and beige overcoat. In between serving his customers and exchanging newspapers or magazines for cash, the man habitually shouted out his sales pitch, "Come and get your papers! Come on! Come and get your papers!"

Right behind the old man, on display inside the booth, I spotted the latest monthly comic edition of the British MI5 Secret Intelligence Agent Alex. I wanted that comic so badly! I had read all the previous Alex agent comics. I locked my feet to the ground and refused to move. "Please, Mum! Please get me that Alex comic!"

As I tugged on Mum's hand, I raised my heels high to observe the comic inside the booth even further. I couldn't believe what I saw. There was a free Super-Agent Alex watch attached to the comic as a free giveaway. Wow! The novelty watch was a replica of the one Alex wore in his comics. It even had the same laser-zapping red button that Alex used to disintegrate all the baddies. "Ah, Mum! Look! It's got a free watch as well! Just like the one Alex wears! Please, can I get it, Mum?"

Mum knew I wouldn't stop pestering her; she was well aware of how much I loved reading the Alex comics. Bob thought they were boring. So, we all queued up at the booth, and Mum purchased the comic for me. Obviously, the first thing I did was carefully peel off the laser-powered MI5 agent watch from the comic, making sure not to rip it in any way. I didn't waste any time and wrapped the watch around my left wrist straightaway. I felt great! As we continued our journey to Nan's house, my eyes glittered with excitement as I gazed at the cover of the comic: 'Whosoever wears this watch will be deemed an agent of the secret intelligence service MI5 and is free to use its plutonium-energy laser-zapping power to destroy all evildoers.' Great! Exactly what I needed.

After Nan and Mum finished their nattering over a good cup of Chai (tea) Mum decided to take us to the library to get some more books. This day couldn't get any better: first came the comic, then the laser-zapping watch, Nan's, and finally our visit to our favourite library!

On route, we had to walk past the skinhead's den. As we got closer, we realised there was a crowd of about twenty skinheads speaking out loud and swearing constantly outside the den. Mum made us all cross the road. She didn't want them to cause us any harm, nor did she want us to hear the rude swearing they indulged in naturally.

"Don't look at them! Keep walking!" Mum warned us, but as always, we couldn't help ourselves and took a peep in the skinheads' direction.

After the library, Mum took us to Rathbone Street Market. She bought us all a 99-flake ice cream cone from the side window of Henry's Cafe. Sharan's ice cream ended up more on her face than in her mouth. Bob and I giggled and munched away as we watched Sharan make a spectacle of herself while she wrestled with her ice cream.

It was great to get out of the house. Whenever we went out on our little trips with Mum, she always made sure that we had a great time and always spoiled us with her treats. She could only imagine the crap we had to face in school; hence, she knew we deserved the treats which gave us a break and diverted our attention away from all that nonsense.

On our way home, as we turned the corner into Rangal Road, we spotted three skinheads, most probably in their late teens, leaning up against the wall. Simultaneously, they all spun their heads in our direction. Mum, unmoved by the skinhead's appearance, gently continued to move Sharan's pram forward. She noticed the fear on my face and grabbed my hand; I tightly held my rolled-up comic in my other hand. Bob had already gripped the pram handle with both hands on the other side of mum. We could all sense danger, except Sharan. She was too busy playing and entertaining herself with her ice-cream-smeared hands.

To get to our house, we had to walk past these skinheads. One skinhead, who was struggling to keep his eyes open and swaying erratically, spoke first, "Oi? Oi? Look, boys! It's a small group of Paki's! Why you Paki's walking the streets? You do know that it's not safe for you Paki's to be walking around freely, don't you?" If that wasn't a direct threat, I don't know what was.

The skinheads purposely stood in front of us and formed a human wall, intentionally blocking us from moving forward. This forced Mum to come to a halt. I raised my head and quickly scanned the faces of the towering skinheads. I didn't recognise none of them. I had never seen them before. It was such a shame that I was only eight years old. I knew very well that I didn't have a chance in hell of fighting these skinheads who were now physically threatening my poor ole' defensive mum. Once again, I wished I was older so that I could have bashed them all up, one by one.

The skinhead wearing the tall red laced shiny boots, that almost reached his kneecaps, began to dig inside his right-hand jeans pocket. As he did this, he suspiciously scanned the surroundings making sure there were no coppers around. I knew this skinhead had made an extra effort in making his red boots shine, it clearly showed. I named him Red-Boots.

"You lot better fuck off back to from wherever yah' fuckin' came from and leave our fuckin' country! Stinking fuckin' Paki's!" As Red-Boots spoke I watched his nostrils pump out air like a steam engine. His eyes grew wider and wider, blazing with fierce rage. I could clearly see and smell his hatred for us. Then Red-Boots surprised us all. When his hand resurfaced from his pocket, we realised he was holding a small penknife. He flicked it open and pointed it toward my mum. The other two skinheads proudly celebrated the actions of their colleague by displaying their horrid grins.

This wasn't the first time that the skinheads had caused trouble with my mum. But what was different about this ambush was the fact that the bastards now actually had the audacity of pointing a knife at her. This I had never seen before. None of us had. It was a different level. It scared the shit out of me and Bob. We both froze up, numbed with fear. Sharan began to cry; she eventually sensed the dangerous atmosphere that surrounded us.

Ah, come on. Let me get this right-three skinheads, one with a knife, harassing a woman who's barely over five feet tall, innocently walking with her baby daughter in a pram and two little boys? *Really?!* Were they even for real? Picking on a poor, innocent, helpless family? I then remembered that this was all part of the holocaust that was coming. This was the beginning; it could not be stopped.

Mum took a deep breath, raised her head, and stared directly at the skinhead with the knife, straight into his eyeballs. She slowly passed the pram to Bob and gently nudged me behind her. This wasn't looking good. She rolled up her sleeves and revealed her massive forearms that she had built after many years of grating onions whilst having made countless Indian dishes.

Whenever the White-British folks heard my mum speak English, they would always purposely ask her another question to confirm and hear how good her English actually was. They simply couldn't believe that an Indian lady wearing Punjabi-Indian customary clothes could speak cockney English so clearly.

My mum was livid after seeing the knife. In an instant, she turned into something that resembled an insane barking dog trying to protect its owners. Mum was as tough as nails when she needed to be.

She let rip with her cockney, "Who'd 'ell d'ya think you're waving that knife at...*BOY*? You think you scare me? 'Ave you even got the bloody guts to use it? Gonna 'arm me and my kids? Well, not on my bloody watch! Yah' bloody blighter!"

I could tell by the quizzical looks on the skinheads' faces that they were all dumbfounded to hear Mum's perfect cockney.

"What? You speak English?" Red-Boots slowly began to lower his knife.

Mum courageously stepped forward, "Yes and for your information, I have spent many years working on the market stalls of East London and dealt with many scummy little shitheads like you on a regular basis! Now, put that knife away and get out of my bloody way, otherwise I am going to clobber yah' earholes while my children watch for entertainment! Go on! Get knotted! Sod off! Sling your hook!"

Wow! Go, Mum, go! Mum wasn't a violent person, but at times like this, she had to make a stand, otherwise only God knows how things would have turned out. The skinheads had discovered they'd chosen the wrong lady to pick on today. Sometimes, I did wonder if Dad was right, and we should have listened to him and stayed home. That way we wouldn't have had to face any of these monsters.

Red-Boots and his two mates backed off; their intimidating tactics had failed utterly. Embarrassed, Red-Boots bravery disintegrated harshly, he slowly closed the penknife and slipped it back into his trouser pocket. Mum had frightened the hell out of these skinheads and startled them with her brave words. Within seconds, they scarpered, vanishing into the nearby alley. Cowards! Mum took Sharan's pram back from Bob and began to march forward with us in pride. Our destination was our home, our 'Little India'.

Swinging her head side to side, looking at me and Bob, she released a warm smile as we all headed toward our front door, "Listen t'me boys. Never, ever show the skinheads that you are scared. You will be, but never show it. Because it will only make them stronger."

We never forgot the great principle and advice that our mum gave us on this day. It did cross my mind that I should have zapped the skinheads with my new MI5 secret agent watch. I concluded that they weren't worth it. I would only be wasting the watch's plutonium energy. I was saving that for the skinhead who had the swastika tattoos on his temples. He was my number one target. I now had a perfect weapon for the approaching holocaust. Hopefully, it would help me to save my family.

A few days later, while he kicked a ball about in our garden, Bob heard me sobbing and sniffing away in our garden boghouse.

He strolled over, "Are you crying in the khazi again, Jag? Who's bullied you this time? Tell me who it is, and I will sort them out!"

I ripped off a sheet of toilet paper and wiped my tears away. I urgently required therapy and support from my brother, "Yes, Bob. I am crying. The Holocaust is coming! We are all going to die!"

"What the hell are you talking about, Jag?" Bob was always, understandably, intrigued by my imagination and thoughts.

"The Nazis! We are surrounded by Nazis! They are eventually going to take us to their concentration camps or even worse, shoot us. They are coming, Bob!"

Bob, astonished by my innocence, shook his head outside the khazi, now highly concerned, "Just come out of the boghouse and we will talk about this. Just bloody stop crying."

Once I came out of the toilet, my nine-year-old brother explained to me that, yes, I was right, all the skinheads were Nazis. However, luckily for us, they did not have any tanks, guns, or concentration camps. He informed me that in this day and time, the Nazi skinheads would not be able to send us to concentration camps. There were now laws set in place to make sure that such atrocities never happened again.

Bob told me that the skinheads were dangerous and followed Hitler's twisted ideals, dreaming of a world ruled by a single, dominant race: the white race. Therefore, yes, we were surrounded by Nazi skinheads and were in danger, but not to the extent that we would be executed outside our front door or taken to any concentration camp. Bob strictly advised me to have a serious break from watching any war-related TV programmes for a while.

It really baffled me during those years when I saw some of the White-British people promote and display the Nazi symbols and flags of Hitler. I mean, had they forgotten that it was their very own relatives who fought against Hitler in the first place? I asked Bob why they did this. Had they forgotten the sacrifices their British ancestors had made during the war? Also, why were the racist white society harassing the Sikhs, when history confirmed that thousands of Sikhs sacrificed their lives by supporting Britain during World War I and World War II? The Sikhs' fierce fighting abilities, bravery and loyalty have been highly praised by many throughout history. Had all this been forgotten? Bob shrugged his shoulders and couldn't provide me with all the answers. It seemed as if I wasn't the only one who was confused with many unanswered questions.

Although it was now clear to me that the German soldiers weren't coming and I wasn't about to be sent to any concentration camp or executed, I was still scared. We were all scared.

The Nazi skinheads lurking around outside our house late at night, like predators, didn't make any of us feel safe at all. We were their prey! After this day, my German-shooting-squad nightmares vanished. Maybe because of the clarification that had been given to me by Bob. Unfortunately for me, there were still plenty more nightmares lurking around in my head that replaced these automatically.

Not only did we have to deal with the skinheads and nightmares, but there were plenty of other challenges that we also had to contend with simultaneously. This included the notorious bullies of Sparrowfield Primary School…

TO BE CONTINUED…

FOR PARENTS, TEACHERS, & GUARDIANS:

TEACHING ABOUT RACISM AND RACIAL HATRED in the UK is a crucial aspect of education that aims to promote understanding, equality, and social cohesion. Schools are increasingly recognising the need to address these issues through an inclusive curriculum that reflects the diverse experiences and contributions of all communities.

This involves not only teaching about historical events related to racism but also fostering racial literacy among students and staff. Educators are encouraged to critically examine existing curricula, incorporate diverse perspectives, and create a school culture that actively challenges discrimination. By addressing racism and racial hatred in schools, the UK education system seeks to equip students with the knowledge and skills to combat prejudice and promote a more equitable society.

The Unbreakable Series is a hard-hitting account demonstrating how racism and racial hatred can manifest themselves in an uneducated society. It's a real-life account of growing up in a society conflicted by rampant racism.

ABOUT THE 'UNBREAKABLE' TRILOGY

Unbreakable – Book 1
Wrong Place, Wrong Time

This deeply vivid and powerful narrative unpacks the events experienced by an Indian family during the 1970s, in East London, when merciless racists roam the streets. Canning Town was the epicentre for the battle between the English National Front and foreign immigrants. Racist ideologies are imprinted on many, which spill out to create widespread prejudice. In the middle of all this carnage is a young Indian boy, Jag Singh and his family. To survive, Jag and his innocent family have no other option and are forced to become unbreakable…

Unbreakable – Book 2
Against All Odds

The trilogy's second instalment depicts the devastating experiences of Jag and his brother Bob. They are surrounded by a predominantly white community where racism is prevalent. The narrative focuses on Jag's attempt to escape bullies as he runs home from school. The story vividly portrays the racial tensions and bullying the brothers face, both at school and in their neighbourhood. Their mother is presented as a fierce protector, confronting teachers when her children are mistreated. The story also highlights the brothers' coping mechanisms, including Jag's use of a toilet shed as his "Fortress of Solitude." The story emphasises the challenges of maintaining cultural identity while integrating into a new society and the family's resilience in the face of discrimination and violence.

Unbreakable – Book 3
The Rise of Monty Singh

In this explosive conclusion to the 'Unbreakable Trilogy', the UK erupts into chaos as racist violence engulfs the nation. Peaceful protests crumble under brutal attacks, forcing Black and Asian communities to fight back in desperate self-defence.

Amidst the turmoil, Jag and his family watch their world unravel on the nightly news. With nowhere to hide and violence closing in, they cling to a fragile hope for salvation.

'Legend: The Final Battle' is a heart-pounding tale of survival against overwhelming odds. As hatred threatens to tear the country apart, Jag's family faces their ultimate test. Will they find a saviour in time, or will they be forced to stand alone against the coming storm?

Brace yourself for a gripping finale that explores the limits of human resilience and the power of unity in the face of division.

ABOUT THE AUTHOR

JAG SINGH IS FROM LONDON, UK, and is an inspirational speaker and writer. He is continuously campaigning in the areas of Anti-Bullying, Mental Health Awareness, and Anti-Hate Crime affecting the well-being of individuals and communities. Having had personal experience of all these challenges and victoriously travelled to the other side, his work now actively supports individuals who encounter such issues.

Jag has volunteered with the NSPCC (The National Society for the Prevention of Cruelty to Children) by conducting seminars and workshops on child protection. He has also hosted, produced, and written various motivational TV and radio shows to inspire others to achieve their goals. He continually writes motivational articles for various internet magazines.

Whilst growing up, Jag faced many challenges, firstly in the 1970s when he had to contend with the racism which was hurled towards him from all directions. Then, during the 1980s he was surrounded by gangland warfare, drug syndicates and criminals. Jag eventually broke free from his hostile childhood environment and started his life again. He enjoys spending time with his family and friends, trains in the martial art of kickboxing, works out in the gym, loves reading, and meditating. He is also fluent in English, Punjabi, Hindi and Urdu.

Jag is on a strong, never-ending mission to leave this world a much better place than he found it.

ACKNOWLEDGEMENTS

WHILE WRITING THESE MEMOIRS, I came across many hurdles and challenges, which I overcame with the kindness and guidance I've received from many great individuals who provided me with their incredible ongoing support.

Firstly, my heart-warming thanks goes to my beloved wife, Emma, and our amazing children, Josh and Alisha for being my strength. They have all kept me motivated and high spirited during the years that I have spent writing these memoirs. Thank you, guys, for your love and encouragement; it would not have been possible without you.

I would also like to thank my elder brother Charanjit Singh AKA 'Bob', for being there for me during our tough school days in the 1970s. Bob also lived and witnessed the nightmare. He tried his utter best to protect me from the brutal racist individuals that surrounded us during that time both inside and outside of school. We will always share these memories of our unfortunate childhood. If it wasn't for you bro' I don't think I would be alive today. I will remain forever grateful for your sacrifices and teachings. Thanks man!

A massive respectful salute goes out to my mum, Prabhjit Kaur and dad, Rajbans Singh, for being brave and spectacular parents considering the dark era we lived through in Canning Town, East London. They both tried and did their best to shelter us from the ever-present dangers that surrounded us at that time. Also, a big thank you goes out to my sister

Sharanjeet Kaur, who, although she was only a baby then, always provided us with a cheeky smile that made the day feel much better than it was.

Many thanks to my uncles and aunts who did their best to educate and protect me and my brother. Despite our challenging childhood, they all taught us how to become law-abiding, loving and educated individuals. Also, thank you guys for filling in those gaps of our family history that I had forgotten or never even knew about; this information was much needed for the completion of this book.

I owe a great deal to my granddad, my dad's dad, Papa Kishan. It's crazy but scary to think that if my dad had listened to the local villagers and never travelled on an aeroplane, and Papa Kishan had not intervened, then I would have never existed! Papa Kishan taught me a lot, and his memories still inspire me up to this very day. I was fortunate to have met him in 1983 when I visited India for the first time at the age of thirteen. Whenever he told me that his village people didn't want my dad to travel in an aeroplane to come to Britain because they thought aeroplanes weren't real and fell out of the sky, he would always roar with laughter. I loved watching him laugh; his shoulders would always bounce away as he chuckled, remembering the barmy villagers and their silly superstitious thoughts. I will never forget the amazing advice that Papa Kishan gave me, "Always think outside the box. That's where you will surely find the answer," thank you Papa Kishan.

I would also like to express my gratitude and respect for the author and publisher, James Minter.

When James first told me that I could become a writer and that I had a remarkable story to share, I thought this would be an impossible task to achieve, as I had buried my past a long time ago. But James advised me that my story would inspire others to reach out and get support, which spurred me to begin my writing journey. James, thanks for helping me make this book a reality with your ongoing support and encouragement.

Wanting to reach a broader audience with my motivational messages, I have written many articles for numerous internet news magazines. I greatly appreciate the support received from all the magazines for publishing my inspirational outpourings, cheers, guys. Also, I want to thank all the people, charities, communities, and organisations that have helped me, and continue to support me in living my dream — spreading the words of hope, inspiration and happiness. And to the many others who've supported me throughout these endeavours — you know who you are — I thank you from the bottom of my heart.

Finally, I would like to thank my two amazing lifelong friends, Lee Bell and Ronnie Kiddell, who have always been there for me and continuously ignited my motivation to write this book. I salute you both!

SUPPORT GROUPS

Organisation	Contact via
Anti-Racist Social Club	Curated & original content resources www.theantiracistsocial.club welcome@theantiracistsocial.club
Samaritans	Whatever you're going through, we will face it with you. www.samaritans.org jo@samaritans.org
Mind	Fighting for mental health, for support, for respect, for you. www.mind.org.uk supportrelations@mind.org.uk
The Mix	Free counselling sessions by phone or webchat for under 25s. Text THEMIX to 85258.
SHERA Research	Researching the impact of domestic abuse/violence on women & children. shera-research@protonmail.com www.shera-research.com
Taraki	Mental health in Punjab communities. www.taraki.co.uk info@taraki.co.uk
Anti-Bullying Alliance	A coalition of organisations & individuals united against bullying aba@ncb.org.uk
NSPCC	Call Childline on 0800 1111
Stop Hate UK	Challenging all forms of hate crime & discrimination: www.stophateuk.org info@Stophateuk.org 0800 1381625

SOCIAL MEDIA

Website: www.jagsingh.uk

X :
https://x.com/jagsingh_ican

Amazon Author Page:
https://www.amazon.co.uk/stores/Jag-Singh/author/B089ZVPZMX

YouTube:
UNBREAKABLE MOTIVATION:

www.youtube.com/c/JagSingh_ican

©UNBREAKABLE
MOTIVATION

For seminars/lectures & guest speaking, contact:
jagsingh70@btinternet.com